Contents

Chapter One	The Eternal Optimist	6
Chapter Two	The Early Years	12
Chapter Three	Moving West	20
Chapter Four	Nancy and Ronnie	26
Chapter Five	Sacramento	34
Chapter Six	Campaigning for the Presidency	42
Chapter Seven	America's Fortieth President	50
Chapter Eight	The President's Second Term	62
Chapter Nine	"My Fellow Americans..."	80
Chapter Ten	The Legacy of Ronald Reagan	86
Chapter Eleven	In Memoriam	90

Chapter One
The Eternal Optimist

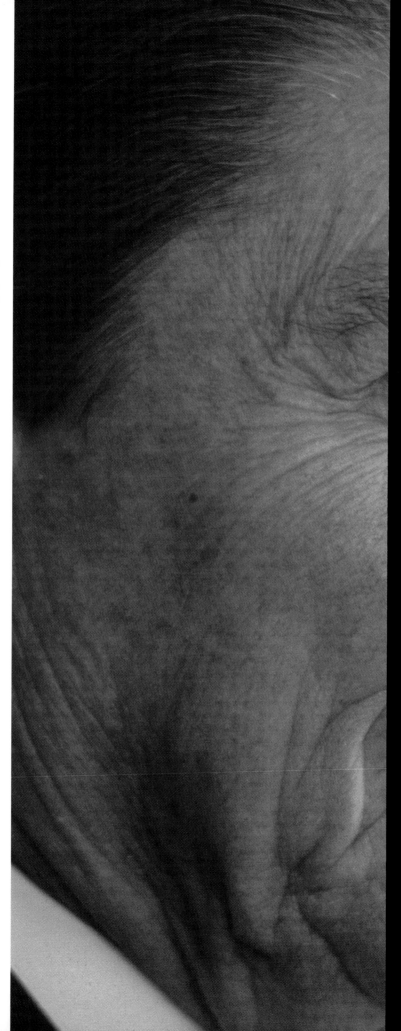

He was tall, built like a football tackle, spoke in a steady tone with a touch of humor when called for—he would one day be dubbed "The Great Communicator"—and with his shock of dark hair and chiseled features, Ronald Wilson Reagan, the fortieth president of the United States, looked as if his visage belonged on Mt. Rushmore.

He was possessed of human decency in abundance in dealings with both world leaders and underlings. He didn't have a mean bone in his body and when on occasion he was disappointed with a staff member's performance, he would be sad rather than angry. What people saw was what they got; there was no "public" Ronald Reagan. He always impressed people with his friendliness and interest in their lives, traits inherited from his mother, Nelle, who never had a bad word to say about anybody. Reagan was particularly adept at putting people at ease; they looked up to him, but he never looked down on them.

There was an air of modesty about him—even a sense of awe—about his new position as president. Consider January 1981, on the evening of his inaugural balls, as the Reagans waited in a holding room at the Washington Hilton. Reagan, resplendent in white tie and tails, caught sight of his reflection in a mirror and began to straighten his tie. Cocking his head, and with the twinkle in his eye that he got whenever he was going to make a grand gesture, he jumped into the air, clicked his heels *a la* Fred Astaire, and exclaimed, "I'm the President of the United States of America!"

REAGAN
A Tribute

He loved to tell light-spirited stories to score important points, many of his anecdotes infused with optimism. One of his favorites was about a family with two children. One child was always down about things, the other always happy, so the parents took both children to a psychiatrist. The doctor put the children in separate rooms, the pessimist surrounded by many new toys, the optimist by a mound of horse manure. After several hours had elapsed, the parents were taken to both rooms. The pessimistic child was in tears, whining that none of the toys were working properly. In the other room, however, the child was laughing as he dug through manure. Astonished, his parents asked, "What are you doing?" And the optimistic child replied, "There must be a pony in here somewhere."

The president could use his formidable communications skills to deliver tougher messages when he deemed necessary. Who can forget his characterization of the Soviet Union as "The Evil Empire," or his dramatic exhortation to the Soviet General Secretary regarding the then-divided Berlin: "Mr. Gorbachev! Tear down this wall"?

There was much more to the man, however, than a physically imposing presence or a way with words. Defying critics all too eager to label him an "amiable dunce," or a "stupid B actor," Reagan demonstrated from an early age that he was intellectually curious and later, as he prepared to enter the political arena, that he had a grasp of the issues—from the intricacies of criminal justice and law enforcement to the complexities of nuclear fission. On meeting the future president for the first time in 1966, just after Reagan's election as governor of California, Edwin Meese III was amazed at Reagan's grasp of concepts the future attorney general had spent his entire professional life working on, as well as by Reagan's ability to assimilate the information, add his own ideas and then formulate his goals for law enforcement in that state. And after he assumed the office of governor, while visiting the Lawrence Livermore Laboratory, a major nuclear research center, Reagan impressed

no less a personage than Dr. Edward Teller, father of the hydrogen bomb and a strong believer in missile defense. Dazzled by the technology he observed at Livermore, Reagan asked many questions. Fifteen years later, as president, Reagan would introduce his Strategic Defense Initiative. While it was broadly based on what he had seen at Livermore, Reagan had decided to exclude the use of nuclear weaponry. As Dr. Teller recalled many years later, "He took our advice but modified it; the modification was his, not ours. He asked questions and, for a long time, did not give the answers...and then he came out with not what had been put into him, but with something better than that."

Ronald Reagan was possessed of great personal courage, as well as the innate sense of humor through which he managed to transcend his apprehensions about his own fate. On March 30, 1981, two months and a few days into his first term

as president, Reagan was shot and critically wounded by John Hinckley Jr. and almost died. As he lay in his hospital bed, he offered some sage advice to his son, Michael: "If you are ever going to be in a position to be shot, don't be wearing a new suit...I understand the parents of the young man who shot me are in the oil business. Do you think just maybe they'd buy me a new suit?" Then in 1985, after being told by his equally courageous First Lady, Nancy, that he had a cancerous tumor in his colon and that it had to be removed immediately, the president reacted by saying, "You mean the bad news is that I don't get to eat supper tonight?"

When Nancy's turn came two years later, however, the President was literally at a loss for words as he was told in the Oval Office by his personal physician that the First Lady likely had breast cancer and would require surgery. He was in total denial and bade the physician goodbye with the words: "I know that you doctors will take care of it." Later that evening, back in the White House family quarters, the president tried to over-compensate by being cheerful, but he couldn't talk about Nancy's condition for several days. The next day, the president said to his physician, "I wish you had stayed up there and given me a good kick. I just couldn't address it."

A momentary veil had come down between the president and his physician. Other associates noticed that as amiable as the president was, when he couldn't deal with an emotional issue an impenetrable curtain would descend. It was likely a protective mechanism he had adopted as a youngster, one that was exacerbated during his Hollywood years and intensified as he was forced to meet the increasing demands of his political life—a sense that if people are at you all the time, you have to hold back something of yourself. In other words, he could be something of a loner, a friendly loner. But he needed Nancy.

Despite his momentary emotional silences, Ronald Reagan knew how to relate to the electorate during his campaign for the presidency. He conveyed his optimistic vision and belief in the American way of life to them at a time of turmoil.

During the administration of Jimmy Carter, military preparedness and U.S. prestige in the world had crumbled, culminating in the taking hostage of sixty-six Americans by Iranian radicals on November 14, 1979. His optimism intensified during his years in the Oval Office and his second campaign was suffused with the concept of a "Mythic America," replete with a stirring campaign commercial proclaiming, "It's Morning Again in America."

Today, as Americans once again aspire to a sense of national pride, pundits and politicians alike—be they Republican, Democratic or Independent—express a certain nostalgia for the wit, grace, courage and optimism of the boy from Dixon, Illinois, who made good first as sportscaster, then as a movie star and communicator, and finally, as the leader of the free world.

A photo, circa 1913, of the John E. Reagan family, taken in Tampico, Illinois. From left are John Reagan, his sons Neil and Ronald, and his wife Nelle Wilson Reagan.

Chapter Two
The Early Years

Ronald Reagan, who would spend eight years residing and working amid the splendors of the White House, was born on February 6, 1911, in a modest, five-room apartment above a bank in the small town of Tampico, Illinois. The second child born to John Edward "Jack" Reagan and the former Nelle Wilson, Ron had an older brother, John Neil, thirty-one months his senior and known affectionately as "Moon."

During Ron's early years, the Reagan family moved from Tampico to Chicago, and then as Jack, a salesman, sought more lucrative employment, to Galesburg in the western part of Illinois. While the Reagans were not poor, they lived modestly in rented apartments and houses. Only after Ron had achieved success as a film actor would Jack and Nelle finally own a home of their own. In his later years, Ron would recall evening meals, consisting of a stew made from a soup bone and peeled vegetables. On Sundays the Reagans would dine "luxuriously" on fried liver.

In Galesburg, Ron—nicknamed "Dutch" by his father because he resembled a "fat Dutchman"—started school, and at age five startled his parents one day by reading the local newspaper. As a youngster, Ron continued to enjoy perusing the papers, as well as reading adventure stories and the Bible. In 1920, in the wake of the growing prosperity that followed the end of World War I, Jack Reagan moved the family to Dixon, a town in northwestern Illinois with a population of about eight thousand. For the first time in his life, Jack had a financial interest in a business as a partner in the Fashion Boot Shop.

Dutch would spend the happiest years of his childhood in Dixon, a close-knit community of merchants and farmers where people knew and cared for one another. There he loved to go swimming, and to fish and hike in the hills above the Rock River, a tributary that flowed into the Mississippi. One of his favorite pastimes was playing cowboys and Indians, a game likely influenced by his love for the western movies of Tom Mix.

In those years, between the World War and the onset of the Great Depression, Ron and Moon enjoyed an almost quintessential Midwestern childhood in Dixon—one characterized by optimism, sense of family, church attendance and community service. Nelle Reagan was noted for her many acts of charity, including visiting prisoners in the local jail and helping them to find employment upon their release.

Yet an unspoken issue marred the boys' sense of security and well-being: Jack Reagan, normally a

loving father and husband, would disappear for days at a time. On one snowy afternoon, Ron arrived home from school to find his father passed out on the front lawn. Picking his father up, the protective Ron carried Jack to his bedroom before Nelle returned from her part-time job. But Nelle was only too aware of Jack's problem—that he was an alcoholic given to sudden drinking bouts and binges.

When sober, Jack taught the boys many important lessons in life. For example, he recounted to them that on one occasion, as he checked into a hotel in a small town in Illinois, the room clerk boasted that Jews were not permitted to stay there. Although it was the only hotel in town and a blizzard was raging outside, Jack decided he could not stay there, spending the night instead in his car. Before he left the hotel, however, Jack made the point of telling the clerk, "I'm a Catholic. If it's come to the point where you won't take Jews, then someday you won't take me either."

Even in the nearly idyllic Dixon, prejudice was common. The local movie house, where Ron spent many afternoons, had segregated seating. Ron and Neil would sit in the all-white orchestra section while blacks were forced to sit in the balcony. Fortunately for the boys, Nelle encouraged them to bring black schoolmates home to play. Ron would learn Jack and Nelle's lessons well; in later life—both as an actor and politician—Ron would strongly oppose any kind of discrimination, be it racial or religious.

At Dixon's Northside High School, Ron was a good student, but lacked confidence on the athletic field, often dropping balls hit to him on the baseball diamond and missing passes during football drills. Then one day, while out for a drive with his parents, he realized that he was profoundly near-sighted. Outfitted with a pair of eyeglasses, Ron was soon excelling at sports. While still in high school, Ron began working as a lifeguard at Lowell Park, a recreation area along the Rock River. He would continue to work there

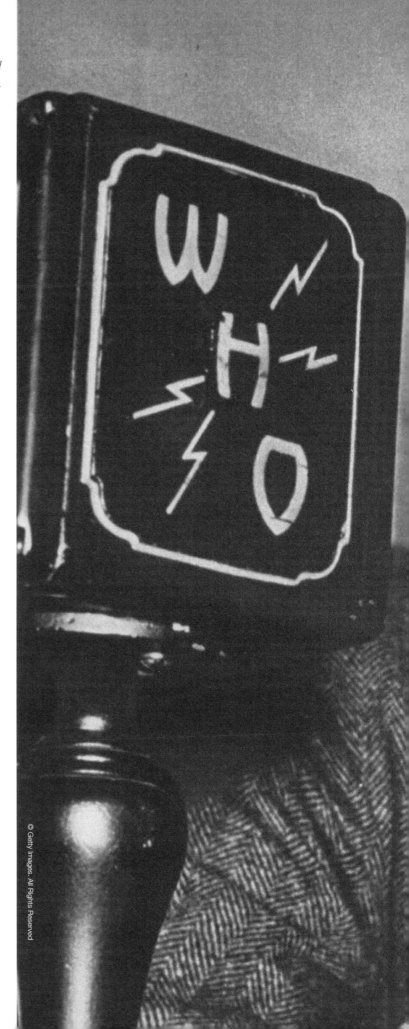

Ronald Reagan as he appeared in 1932 when he worked as a sportscaster for WHO radio in Des Moines, Iowa.

for the next seven summers, rescuing seventy-seven people.

It was at Northside, while studying English with a new teacher, B.J. Frazer, that Ron developed his interest in acting. Frazer's students would read aloud essays they had written. Ron's were humorous, generating laughter and giving him the confidence to try out for a school play. By his senior year, Ron was "addicted" to theater, learning under Frazer's wise tutelage to empathize with the character he portrayed.

After graduating from Northside, Ron received a partial athletic scholarship from Eureka College, a small liberal arts school in central Illinois which was operated by the Disciples of Christ. During his years there, Reagan would supplement that student aid by working at various campus jobs and by tapping his savings from his earnings as lifeguard to pay the annual $350 fee for tuition, room and board.

At Eureka, Ron found his second acting mentor, Ellen Marie Johnson, an English professor who served as faculty adviser for theater arts. Johnson somehow persuaded Northwestern University to allow Eureka to compete in its prestigious one-act play contest, in which her students would be going up against such institutions as the Ivy League universities Princeton and Yale. Ron, who played a shepherd in Edna Vincent Millay's anti-war play, *Aria da Capo*, was one of three performers to win an award and Eureka came in second in the overall competition.

During his senior year at Eureka, Ron became fascinated by radio, and was particularly interested in sports broadcasting. When in the privacy of his room, he often emulated the styles of famed sportscasters Ted Husing and Graham McNamee. Then, following his graduation in June 1932, Ron traveled to Chicago, where he wrangled an appointment with the program

May Robson, Reagan and Priscilla Lane in a scene from the feature film Million Dollar Baby, *directed by Vincent Sherman, 1941.*

director of the local NBC affiliate but was told that he lacked the experience necessary to work there and was advised to try to break into radio with a smaller station.

Leaving Dixon in the family's ancient Oldsmobile, he drove over the Mississippi to Davenport, Iowa, where he was hired as a temporary announcer, his assignment to broadcast four University of Iowa football games. For his efforts, radio station WOC would pay him five dollars for the first game and ten dollars for each of the next three. An instant success, Ron was hired on a permanent basis at the seemingly generous salary of $100 per month. Soon, WHO, a Des Moines station that had just received a permit to broadcast at 50,000 watts, absorbed the WOC staff and Reagan's salary was increased to seventy-five dollars per week. As WHO joined the 15 or so 50,000 watt clear channel stations across the U.S., Ron's voice could be heard far outside of Iowa.

In the spring of 1937, Ron persuaded the station's management to allow him to accompany the Chicago Cubs to their Catalina Island, California, training base. He had broadcast hundreds of Cub games using a technique so immediate that listeners often thought he was present at Wrigley Field when, in reality, he was reading accounts of the action from the newsroom's wire service ticker.

One evening, Ron took the ferry into Los Angeles to have dinner with Joy Hodges, a singer he had met in Des Moines with whom he had remained friends. She set up an appointment for Ron with Bill Meiklejohn, a well-known Hollywood agent. The sports announcer with the gift for drama was about to find another calling.

Chapter Three
Moving West

Ronald Reagan's film career, which included 51 appearances spanning two decades, began with a five-minute screen test as he and a young actress read from *The Philadelphia Story*. Bill Meiklejohn, the agent who had arranged the test, believed Reagan to be another Robert Taylor—he was the handsome leading man who had played opposite many of the leading ladies of the thirties and forties. While Ron never quite achieved Taylor's level of stardom, he was featured in a number of highly successful films and his performances were generally well regarded.

Ron's career had gotten off to an odd start. As soon as the screen test was completed, he boarded a train for Des Moines, where he was due to begin broadcasting Cubs games. Within hours after his arrival in Iowa, Ron received a telegram from Meiklejohn informing him that Warner Bros. had offered him a seven-year contract. A month later, Ron moved to California where, in a matter of days, he was acting in his first film, *Love is on the Air*. Quite aptly, he was cast as a radio announcer.

The *Hollywood Reporter*'s review of the film appeared to confirm Meiklejohn's prophecy. It stated: "*Love is on the Air* presents a new leading man, Ronald Reagan, who is a natural, giving one of the best first picture performances Hollywood has offered in many a day." Warner Bros. renewed Ron's contract, raising his salary a few days after the review's appearance. Although he made eight films in his first year as an actor, he would never reach the top rank of Hollywood's male stars.

He is remembered, however, for his portrayal of George Gipp, the famed football hero who died two weeks before his team's final game, in *Knute Rockne—All American.* Playing opposite Pat O'Brien, an established star, as Rockne, Ron made the most of the opportunity afforded him in that relatively small part. In a scene that would become legendary, Gipp pleads with his coach, "Some day when things are tough and the breaks are going against the boys, ask them to go in there and win one for the Gipper."

Knute Rockne gave a great boost to Reagan's career, leading to a large increase in both salary and prestige, and opened the way for him to star in films featuring some of Hollywood's finest actors and actresses, including Errol Flynn, Wallace Beery, and Ann Sheridan. His performance as George Gipp also led to his being cast in *King's Row,* which was made in 1941. Playing a double amputee, Ron more than held his own against Ms. Sheridan and the highly regarded Charles Coburn. Ron believed *King's Row* to have been his best film.

Following his notable appearance in *King's Row,* Ron appeared to be on the verge of major stardom. Then, in the wake of the bombing of Pearl Harbor by the Japanese at year's end, Hollywood, like the rest of the nation, went on a war footing. Ron, who in 1937 had enrolled as a Second Lieutenant in the Army Officers Reserve Corps cavalry, received a notice in January 1942 to report for active duty. His poor eyesight precluded overseas duty. Assigned instead to an army unit based in Culver City, California, Ron participated in the production of training and propaganda films. It was while assigned there that Ron became one of the first Americans to learn of the horrors of the Nazi Holocaust when he viewed footage his unit received that had been shot in a death camp.

Following the war's end, Ron was cast in a number of films, and from the late forties to the early fifties, he had to compete with much younger actors for starring roles. Thus he never lived up to his early potential. He assumed a major non-acting role in the industry, however. Appointed in 1938 to

the board of the Screen Actors Guild—known in the industry as SAG—Ron became an activist in the union, which represents thousands of actors in their negotiations with the large studios. And in 1947, he was elected its president, a responsibility he would fulfill for five consecutive terms.

Ron's personal life during the forties had its share of both joy and disappointment. In 1940, he had married actress Jane Wyman, then also under contract to Warner Bros. Their union, much bally-hooed by the studio's public relations department, would end in mutual recriminations eight years later, in 1948, the same year Ms. Wyman starred in *Johnny Belinda*, the role for which she won the Oscar for Best Actress in 1949. Despite their problems, the couple did have a daughter, Maureen, now deceased, and adopted a son, Michael. Both children were steadfast in their loyalty to their father.

While president of SAG, Ron was forced to confront growing allegations that communists had gained considerable influence in the film industry. Testifying before the House Un-American Activities Committee, he was considered a friendly witness. Yet, despite his abhorrence of communism, Ron opposed unofficial blacklists, which had ruined the careers of a number of Hollywood personalities. As he told the committee, "I hope that we are never prompted by fear of communism into compromising our democratic principles." Still, Ron was troubled by the overall threat that communism posed to the nation. He knew from personal experience with SAG that attempts at communist infiltration of the industry were not uncommon. In his autobiography, *An American Life*, Ron summed up his views on the issue: "I knew from the experience of hand-to-hand combat that America faced no more insidious evil or threat than that of communism."

One fateful, unanticipated outcome of his struggle with communists in Hollywood was his meeting with Nancy Davis, a starlet then under contract to MGM. Her name had been placed on the

rosters of several communist front organizations, and her friend, the director Mervyn LeRoy, asked Ron to look into the possibility that there might be two actresses named Nancy Davis. Ron, in his capacity as SAG's president, delved into the matter, discovering that MGM's Nancy Davis was not involved in the front groups' activities. Reagan then called LeRoy and informed him that Nancy had been cleared. The director, however, knowing of Nancy's anxiety concerning the issue, suggested that Ron take her to dinner in order to reassure her that all was well.

As Ronald Reagan and Nancy Davis entered the restaurant that evening, they could hardly imagine what lay ahead.

Reagan, right, actress Nancy Davis, center, and actor Arthur Franz talk during filming of the 1957 movie Hellcats of the Navy.

Chapter Four
Nancy and Ronnie

When Ron called Nancy Davis late on that fateful afternoon in the fall of 1949 and suggested they meet that evening at Mervyn LeRoy's suggestion, he gave himself a convenient escape: he had an early call the next morning, thus it would have to be an abbreviated evening. Although she had no such excuse, Nancy had her pride and so she replied in kind. When Ron arrived at her door at 7:30 to escort her to LaRue's on the Sunset Strip—the place to be seen—she was relieved to see that Ronald Reagan looked as handsome in person as he did on the screen.

After discussing her problem briefly—Ron suggested that Nancy change her last name, she refused, and he promised to help clear her name—their conversation turned more social. Ron's excellent sense of humor was very much in evidence that fateful night. One thing that particularly impressed Nancy was that the tall, handsome actor, unlike many of his colleagues, didn't talk about himself, speaking passionately instead about how much SAG meant to him, of how much he enjoyed his ranch, horses, and wine, and of how interested he was in the Civil War. By the end of that evening—Ron had forgotten about his "early call" the moment he laid eyes on the starlet —Nancy was calling the president of SAG "Ronnie."

Soon thereafter, with fellow film star William Holden and his wife, Ardis, in attendance as best man and matron of honor, respectively, Nancy and Ronnie exchanged their wedding vows on March 4, 1952, in the Little Brown Church in the Valley. After spending their wedding night at a nearby hotel, the Reagans departed for Phoenix, Arizona, where Nancy made her first telephone call as a married woman, to room serv-

ice: "This is Mrs. Ronald Reagan," she exclaimed, with more than a hint of pride and happiness.

While they were very much in love, the Reagans' first year of married life would prove to be quite difficult. His film roles had almost evaporated and thus Nancy, who in anticipation of marriage and motherhood had been released from her seven-year contract at MGM, had to return to work for a time in order to help make ends meet. Ronnie already had two children to support from his marriage to Jane Wyman, Maureen, born in 1941, and Michael, born and adopted in 1946. Nancy, inexperienced in dealing with a husband, let alone children, was thrust immediately into a trying situation. As she would recall many years later in her memoir, *My Turn*, "I became a parent the day I married Ronnie...It's not easy to marry a man who already has children." Then in the fall of 1952, Nancy gave birth to her own child, Patti, followed six years later by Ron Jr. She found her new role the most difficult of her life; as she would acknowledge in *My Turn*, "I was an insecure mother." Nancy's early unease, coupled with both the normal demands of married life and their own special circumstances—dealing with the effects of a "blended" family of high-spirited children while maintaining their public profiles—would have repercussions on their children, especially Patti, who for many years resented her father for having embarked on his political career. On the November evening in 1966 when Ronnie called his fourteen-year-old daughter, who was away at boarding school in Arizona, to tell her that he had just been elected governor of California, the teenager burst into tears, then told him that she was upset with his "establishment" views.

While Maureen, Michael, and Ron Jr. also had issues with Nancy and Ronnie from time to time, their relations with their parents were less troubled than Patti's were. Maureen and Michael would prove to be valued political advisers and Ron Jr., who became a professional dancer and broadcasting personality with more than a touch of the Reagan charm, would make his parents proud.

While tensions between parents and children can often drive a husband and wife apart, the Reagans' difficulties with their children, played out most often in the very public glare of the Washington spotlight, would cause Nancy and Ronnie to draw closer. At times it appeared that Ron needed only Nancy—a circumstance reflected in his public life too—and Nancy lived only for Ronnie.

Whereas Ronnie's affection and devotion would be viewed by many of his admirers as desirable, even noble, and even his seeming reluctance to stand up to Nancy when he disagreed with her views or behavior would be explained away, her constant attention to his every need, coupled with fierce protectiveness, would be criticized by her detractors. She would be portrayed by her critics as extravagant, manipulative, meddling—a latter-day Lady Macbeth—and downright mean to those who stood in her way.

In fact, while Ronnie was openly adoring and dependent on his Nancy, he could express displeasure with her views, as he did during the controversy over his visit to a cemetery in Germany, near the town of Bitburg, where, it was revealed during planning for the trip, members of the Second Waffen SS Panzer division, who had massacred 642 French civilians in June 1944, were buried. Nancy felt very strongly that Ronnie should cancel his trip to Bitburg. He refused, as he had promised the German chancellor, Helmut Kohl, that he would go there. To Ronnie, a promise was a promise. As late as two days before his departure for Germany, Nancy made one more attempt to alter his schedule. Ronnie's White House deputy chief of staff, Michael Deaver, on his way to Germany as part of the president's advance team, was actually enroute to Andrews Air Force Base, when he was called back to the White House for an emergency meeting with the president. Ushering Deaver into his den and closing the door, Ronnie said to his trusted aide, "I know you and Nancy don't want me to go through with this, but..." And that was that. On another occasion, when Nancy felt that Ronnie should tone down his anti-Soviet rhetoric, he told her, very firmly, to stop talking.

One aspect of Nancy's behavior that Ronnie never took issue with—one that would generate much gossip and controversy during the White House years—was her dependence for some time on the services of an astrologer, Joan Quigley. Nancy had become aware of Quigley during the 1980 presidential campaign. The astrologer had contacted her, making the comforting prediction that Ronnie would win in November and offering to send a written account of things they should be on the lookout for during the last three months of the campaign.

Accepting the astrologer's offer at that stressful time in her and Ronnie's political quest, Nancy would again turn to Quigley following the attempt on Ronnie's life. He never took issue with their relationship. Ronnie likely understood the enormous stresses faced by politicians' spouses. Nancy and Quigley would eventually part company.

Once the news of Nancy's relationship with her astrologer had been revealed by the disgruntled former cabinet member and White House chief of staff Donald Regan, there was a firestorm of criticism of Nancy. Her critics had already savaged the svelte and glamorous First Lady for her taste in clothes; her seeming extravagance in buying new china for the White House; being over-protective of Ronnie; opting for the most radical surgery available for breast cancer; adopting causes with trite messages; and, most egregiously, for what was perceived as her meddling and manipulation of the seemingly docile and detached president. In fact, Nancy thought it her duty to dress well and to promote the clothing of American designers; she did purchase new china because the White House collection was chipped and discolored; she raised public consciousness about breast cancer, courageously electing to have a radical mastectomy in the face of feminist criticism; she made the public more aware of the terrible pressures faced by youngsters with her dramatic "Just Say No To Drugs" campaign; she did protect Ronnie, because she understood her roll as a buffer; and she did speak out when she thought the president was being ill-served, not because he was detached and docile.

In the wake of the former president's announcement that he suffered from Alzheimer's Disease, Nancy proved yet again her outstanding devotion to her beloved Ronnie. She rarely left him overnight unless she had a politically related obligation, and then only most reluctantly. While Alzheimer's tragically robbed Ronald Reagan of his memories of their long life together, they live on with Nancy.

Chapter Five
Sacramento

From the late forties to the early fifties, Ronald Reagan, no longer under contract to Warner Bros. and thus without a guaranteed income, made ten films, including the much derided *Bedtime for Bonzo*, in which a chimpanzee stole the film. He achieved some critical success playing famed baseball pitcher Grover Cleveland Alexander in *Winning Team*, but his career was definitely in a downward cycle. Newly married and in need of a more adequate income, Reagan took a job as a master of ceremonies in a Las Vegas nightclub. Then, in 1954, Taft Schreiber, a major executive at Music Corporation of America, offered him a new role, one that would set him on the course that would lead to the presidency.

Reagan became the host of the *General Electric Theater*, which each Sunday evening featured a half-hour-long play, often starring Oscar winners and other established Hollywood stars. In fulfilling his responsibilities, Reagan traveled to General Electric plants throughout the country, visiting 139 facilities in thirty-nine states during his eight years with the company, where he met, and spoke with, more than 250,000 General Electric employees.

In speaking with workers on assembly lines and in offices, Reagan would articulate his philosophy that individuals and private groups, rather than the government, could accomplish more good for society. His speeches, in which he warned people about the excesses of government, began to attract attention beyond General Electric and he was soon receiving invitations to address civic and business organizations, his observations often quoted in the media.

The political content of Reagan's speeches, as well as his strident anti-communist message, offended certain *GE Theater* viewers and consumers of the corporation's products. In 1962, following a change in General Electric's management, he was asked to tone down his message and to devote his remarks to the marketing of the company's products. When he refused to do so, the *GE Theater* was cancelled. That was the least of Reagan's woes in 1962, however. His beloved mother, Nelle, died from the effects of a devastating illness that would several years later be identified as Alzheimer's disease. Some years later, his older brother, Neil, would succumb to Alzheimer's.

Following the loss of his position with General Electric, and the considerable income it had generated, Reagan attempted to revive his film career. Cast for the first time as a villain, in a remake of the 1946 box office hit *The Killers*, he disappointed fans who had been accustomed to seeing him in sympathetic roles. With the film's critical and financial failure, he would turn once again to television, becoming the host of *Death Valley Days*.

By that time, Reagan was becoming increasingly active on the national political scene, having registered as a Republican in 1962, following his departure from General Electric. He had previously been a long-time Democrat, having supported Helen Gahagan Douglas in 1950 during her controversial Senate campaign against Richard Nixon. In 1952, he joined other Democrats in supporting Dwight Eisenhower in his first presidential bid. Then in 1960, he supported Nixon in his campaign against John F. Kennedy.

In 1964, Reagan would play a pivotal role in Barry Goldwater's campaign against the incumbent president, Lyndon Johnson. As co-chairman of Goldwater's California effort, Reagan traveled the state, attacking Johnson's "Great Society" programs. In August, addressing an audience of eight hundred at the Coconut Grove, a Los Angeles nightclub, he accused the Democrats of "taking the nation on the road to socialism." To Ronald

Reagan, America was at a crossroads, needing to choose between continuing the mistakes of the Kennedy and Johnson years or "fighting to reclaim the liberties being taken from us."

Immediately following the speech, Reagan was asked by a small group of wealthy Goldwater supporters whether he would be willing to repeat it on television, provided the funds could be raised to purchase airtime. He agreed to do so, the funds were secured and his address, which has gone down in Reagan lore as "The Speech," was taped before a live audience of Republicans in Los Angeles. Aired nationwide on October 27, "The Speech" was a sensation; the switchboard at the headquarters of the Republican National Committee was deluged with calls and pledges of more than one million dollars to the Goldwater campaign.

HELP
CLEAN UP
THE MESS
IN
SACRAMENTO!

Reagan, a candidate for the Republican nomination for governor of California, is all smiles as he returns a poster to one of his supporters after signing his autograph at the Sacramento airport on June 6, 1966. Reagan was on a six-city, primary election eve campaign trip, shoring up party support for his successful bid for the November gubernatorial election.

While Reagan's stirring call to action failed to stem Johnson's overwhelming victory, his presence on the political scene was established: He was now the Republican to be reckoned with. As he would write nearly thirty years later in his memoir, *An American Life*, "...that speech was one of the most important milestones in my life—another one of those unexpected turns in the road that led me on a path I never expected to take."

That path would lead to Reagan's candidacy in 1966 for the governorship of California against the two-term incumbent, Edmund "Pat" Brown Jr., the Democrat who had seemingly sent Richard Nixon into political oblivion in 1962. In November 1966, Reagan, the perceived underdog, was elected governor in a landslide; he had defeated Brown by nearly one million votes.

The former sportscaster-turned-film star now turned his attention to running the nation's most populous state, one wracked by budget deficits and growing student unrest. To many pundits, the distance from Hollywood to Sacramento was viewed as being far greater than the approximately 400 miles between the two cities.

Although Californians had previously elected a former actor to high office—having sent George Murphy to the U. S. Senate in 1964—Reagan's critics could not imagine how the newly elected governor, with his anti-government, pro-business philosophy, could effectively govern a state as diverse and complex as California. That would be the first time, but not the last, that Ronald Reagan's political capabilities would be underestimated. During the campaign, candidate Reagan had pledged to produce "A Creative Society." Now, as Governor Reagan, he set about streamlining the state's government, appointing well-qualified people to key positions. By the end of his first term, he had not only cut the large state deficit but had actually created a surplus, resulting in tax rebates to millions of residents.

For Governor...
Ronald
REAGAN
For Governor...
Ronald
REAGAN
For Governor...
Ronald
REAGAN

Reagan purses his lips April 3, 1970 as he listens to Irving Hall, a graduate student at UC Riverside during a discussion at the Western Political Science Association meeting in Sacramento. Hall accused Reagan of "expressing a philosophy which has no relevance to power politics in California."

Reagan's responsibilities as governor were complicated by the Democratic majority in the legislature, led ably by the speaker, Jesse Unruh. In his book *Ronnie and Jesse: A Political Odyssey*, Reagan's biographer, Lou Cannon, captures the essence of the rivalry between the two politicians. Their first great battle, in which Reagan would emerge the victor, concerned tuition at the University of California. In 1970, Reagan would beat back Unruh's attempt to wrest the governorship from him. Two years earlier, Reagan had made his first bid to win the Republican presidential nomination, an error in judgment that would lead him to more carefully calibrate his next run for national office.

The issue that best defined Reagan's handling of difficult issues concerned the increasingly militant student unrest at the University of California's nine campuses, which initially sprang from a variety of causes—from the students' sense of alienation, the hugeness of the university, and the perception that the faculty were more interested in pursuing research than in teaching and in developing relationships with their students. Later, the escalating war in Vietnam would spark further, and often violent, protests. Governor Reagan, who in his campaign had warned protesting student activists to "obey the law or get out"—he believed that most of the student body were opposed to the demonstrations—reacted by calling in the National Guard to restore order.

In 1974, toward the end of his largely successful second term, the governor of California resisted entreaties of movers and shakers in the state's Republican Party that he seek a third term. By now, Ronald Reagan had sights set on 1600 Pennsylvania Avenue.

SENATOR HOTEL

Former president Gerald Ford, left, lends his support to fellow Republican and presidential candidate Reagan and running mate George Bush, seen here on the final day of campaining in Peoria, Illinois on November 3, 1980.

Chapter Six
Campaigning for the Presidency

Out of office for the first time in eight years, Reagan maintained his political visibility through frequent speaking dates, a syndicated newspaper column, and a radio commentary. In late 1975, he announced his candidacy for the Republican presidential nomination.

He would have an uphill battle against the incumbent, Gerald Ford, a former congressman from Michigan and long-time moderate who had been the Republican minority leader in the House of Representatives before being selected by Nixon to succeed the disgraced Spiro Agnew as vice president. Succeeding Richard Nixon following the president's resignation in August 1974, Ford retained Henry Kissinger as secretary of state, thus signaling his intention to continue Nixon's policy of détente with the Soviet Union.

In entering the race against Ford, Reagan encountered stiff opposition from Republican leaders, including many governors and mayors. As the 1976 election approached, the last thing those politicians desired was a further split in their already severely diminished party, whose effectiveness had been undermined by both the Watergate scandal and by Ford's controversial pardon of his predecessor.

As the campaign for the nomination got under way, Ford appeared to be in a strong position to be the party's candidate. But he only narrowly defeated Reagan in the New Hampshire Primary. Then, in late March, just before the North Carolina Primary,

Reagan went on national television to deliver a blistering attack on Ford's foreign policy. In Reagan's view, confrontation with the USSR, rather than détente, would assure victory in the decades-old cold war. When Reagan swept to victory in North Carolina, he appeared on the way to winning his party's nomination. While Ford recovered his momentum, defeating Reagan at the Republican Convention in Kansas City, Reagan had made a strong showing, winning more than 47 percent of the delegates' votes. In a show of unity following the first ballot, Reagan ascended the platform and asked the delegates to make Ford's nomination unanimous. More significant for his future, however, was Reagan's address to the convention, one that identified him as the Republican Party's strongest post-1976 candidate should Ford lose that election.

With former Georgia Governor Jimmy Carter's victory in 1976 returning the presidency to the Democrats, Reagan began to formulate his strategy for 1980, putting together a team for that year's campaign and articulating his own political philosophy in appearances throughout the United States. As Reagan pursued his agenda, events were taking place outside the United States that would have a profound impact upon the Carter presidency.

In 1978, the militant Muslim cleric, Ayatollah Khomeini, returned to Iran from exile in France, overthrew the United States' long-time ally, Shah Reza Pahlevi, and established a fundamentalist Islamic regime. In Nicaragua the following July, the forty-three-year reign of strongman Anastasio Somoza came to an end when his government was overthrown by the Marxist Sandinista movement, which was closely allied with the Cuban dictator Fidel Castro. While the Sandinistas had initially pledged to institute democratic reforms, they soon instituted a series of repressive measures, and threatened to export their political philosophy throughout Latin America.

Later that year, two dramatic events would fur-

ther test the Carter administration's capability and prestige internationally. On November 4, 1979, sixty-six Americans were taken hostage at the U.S. Embassy in Tehran by Islamic radicals; then on December 29, Afghanistan was invaded by Soviet troops. Carter's response to both crises appeared weak and inappropriate. In the first instance, his administration's attempt at a military rescue of the hostages failed when one of the helicopters that had been deployed to the Iranian desert was downed in a sandstorm and there were no backup aircraft on hand to complete the mission. Then, in response to the Soviet Union's aggression in Afghanistan, Carter refused to allow U.S. athletes to participate in the 1980 Moscow Olympics. The move had little impact on the Soviets, though their campaign against Afghanistan, which would escalate into an extremely bloody conflict, was regarded by many as their own Vietnam.

As Reagan prepared to run in the 1980 Republican primaries, he faced serious opposition from several seasoned politicians. They included former Congressman, CIA director and U.N. Ambassador George Bush; Senate Minority Leader Howard Baker; former Governor and Secretary of the Treasury John Connally; Senator Robert Dole, and ten-term Congressman John Anderson, who would eventually run as an Independent. Reagan hired his 1976 campaign manager, John Sears, to lead his 1980 effort. Sears replaced key members of Reagan's California inner circle, much to the dismay of Nancy, Michael, and their close friends. As the race for the nomination got under way, Reagan, his political team, family and friends were all shocked by his defeat in the Iowa caucuses.

Following Reagan's loss in Iowa, winning the New Hampshire primary was crucial—it was the primary that would make or break the Reagan campaign. On the eve of the election, Reagan, never one to fire staff easily, learned that Sears was threatening to replace his long time close aide and confidante, Edwin Meese. Calling Sears

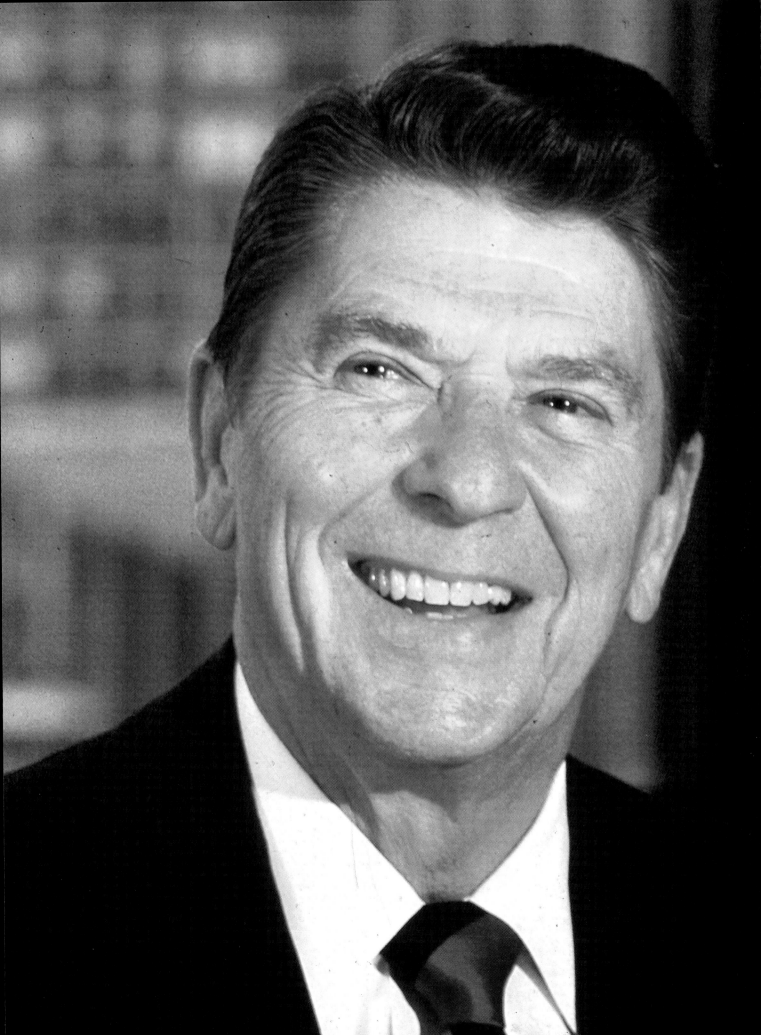

in, Reagan demanded his resignation. That decisive move by Reagan, which led to the appointment of Wall Street lawyer William Casey as his campaign manager—Casey would be appointed director of the Central Intelligence Agency by President Reagan—was instrumental in securing his victory in New Hampshire, thus assuring his candidacy. And on July 17, at the Republican National Convention in Detroit, he was nominated on the first ballot.

With his nomination in hand, Reagan and his staff turned their attention to the list of potential running mates. There followed one of the strangest incidents in the history of the American presidential nominating process: as Reagan and his aides vetted various names, a small group of moderate Republicans, led likely by Henry Kissinger, schemed to obtain the vice presidential nomination for former President Gerald Ford. The Kissinger people, speaking of a "dream ticket," called attention to polling data suggesting that Reagan could only defeat Jimmy Carter with Ford as his running mate. Reagan's advisers, annoyed and dismayed at the blatant lobbying for Ford, were outraged when it appeared that Ford would accept second spot on the ticket, but with one condition: that he would become the de facto co-president, with unprecedented foreign policy influence and responsibilities.

To Reagan's team, the initiative on Ford's behalf implied that their man was incapable of governing the nation on his own. Reagan was himself not only uncomfortable with the Kissinger-led cabal, but deeply offended by the suggestion that he lacked presidential gravitas. However, he was willing to meet with Ford. After their hour-long session in Reagan's hotel suite, the two men emerged in good humor, and Reagan told his advisers, "We both agreed this wasn't going to work. It was simply the right thing to do."

Almost immediately, Reagan turned to his trusted aide, Michael Deaver, who had been with him since the Sacramento years, and said, "Get Bush on the phone." The Bush people, winding down after the strenuous campaign, were shocked when Reagan asked their leader to be his running mate. Bush was actually convinced that Reagan had already selected Gerald Ford when the phone rang and Reagan asked him to join the ticket. Another aide, sent by Reagan to the Bush suite to personally convey the candidate's message, would later recall: "It was like walking into a fraternity house at about two o'clock on a Sunday morning, after a big party."

While Bush was reputed to have the best resume in Washington, not all of Reagan's supporters were delighted with his selection. Bush had offended many Republicans with his characterization of the presidential candidate's fiscal policies as "voodoo economics," and his moderate views on abortion and other domestic policy issues worried many on the Republican right. When evangelist Billy Graham telephoned the activist pastor Jerry Falwell, the founder and head of the Moral Majority, who is now a close friend of Bush's but then had reservations about him, to ask if he was upset about Bush's having joined the ticket, Falwell replied, "Billy, I'll just pray that God will give Ronald Reagan eight years of wonderful health."

The fall campaign would prove to be particularly acrimonious, with Carter attempting to paint his opponent as a political extremist whose fiscal policies would endanger social security and welfare, and Reagan calling attention to the failings of the Carter administration, characterizing them as a "litany of broken promises." In his effort to cast his opponent as a weak, ineffectual commander in chief, Reagan was inadvertently helped by Carter's staff, who had prepared a list of the 660 promises Carter had made during the 1976

President Jimmy Carter, left, and Republican Presidential candidate Reagan shake hands Tuesday night, October 28, 1980, in Cleveland, Ohio, prior to debating before a nationwide television audience.

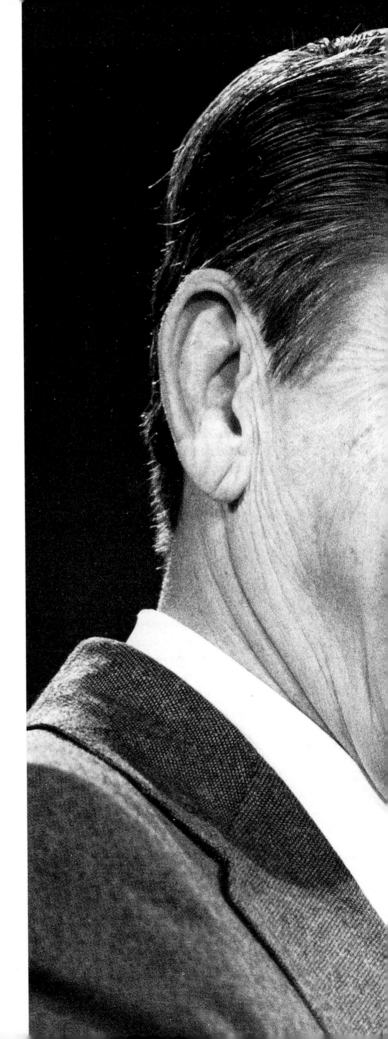

campaign. The campaign's decisive moment occurred on October 24, 1980, when, during their sole debate, Reagan, who had throughout the campaign accused Carter of distorting his record, succeeded in countering Carter's claim that he, Reagan, would weaken Medicare. Looking his opponent squarely in the eye, then pausing for effect, Reagan exclaimed in a tone of good-humored exasperation, "There you go again."

Election Day, November 4, 1980, was nearly anti-climatic. Reagan swept to victory, carrying forty-four states, winning fifty-one per cent of the popular vote to Carter's forty-one per cent and Anderson's seven per cent. The dimension of Reagan's victory gave the Republicans control of the Senate, that outcome made possible in part by the Moral Majority's registration drive among evangelical Christians, a development that fore-shadowed the influence of the "religious right" in presidential elections to come.

At five o'clock that afternoon, candidate Reagan was in the shower, getting ready for his traditional election-evening private dinner with friends before making his way to his campaign headquarters, when Nancy called out, "Honey, the president is on the phone." Responding, Reagan asked, "Can you tell him I'm in the shower?" Nancy said, "I told him, but he needs to talk to you."

Standing there, with a towel wrapped around him, saying, "Yes, Mr. President..." Ronald Reagan, the man who had defied his critics by making the transition from celluloid to Sacramento and from there to his nomination to the nation's highest office, learned that he had won the presidency. Uttering his first words as president-elect, the modest, affable Ronald Wilson Reagan exclaimed, "Well, I'll be..."

Chapter Seven
America's Fortieth President: His First Term

During the period of transition between the end of Carter's presidency and Reagan's ascension to power, the new commander in chief assembled the top echelon of his administration. As he had done in Sacramento, Reagan wished to surround himself with competent staff, aides he could trust with significant responsibility. While as president he would be in command, he preferred to concentrate on the larger picture, leaving day-to-day issues to his subordinates. Thus he brought in such long-time loyalists as Michael Deaver as deputy chief of staff and Edwin Meese III as his counselor. He did, however, choose an outsider, James Baker III, a Texas lawyer close to both Ford and Bush, as chief of staff.

Reagan's administrative style was distinct from those of his predecessors. Eisenhower, a product of the military's chain of command, required his aides to prepare one-page memoranda on key issues; Kennedy relied on a revolving group of "wise men"— comprised of former Democratic Party office holders and intellectuals—as well as on his brother, Robert, to advise in decision-making; Johnson, who could not stand the idea of delegating authority, spent hours poring over maps in selecting targets for U.S. air strikes against North Vietnam; Nixon closeted himself in a small hideaway office in the Old Executive Office Building, where he wrote his policy formulations on legal-size yellow pads; and Carter, a nuclear engineer by training, became caught up in the minutiae of the presidency, spending many long nights

President Reagan, with his newly-named Middle East envoy, Donald Rumsfeld, right, defends the use of U.S. troops in Grenada during a November. 3, 1983 press briefing at the White House.

alone in the Oval Office, deciding on whom to appoint to such posts as federal district court judgeships and mid-level administration staff.

While Reagan could delegate authority, he chose to oversee a number of major concepts he brought to his new position, concerning both domestic and foreign policy. He was, in fact, the most ideologically oriented president of the last half of the twentieth century, opposing the spread of communism, favoring private enterprise, and valuing the individual's role in creating a just society. While many of his critics have characterized Reagan's approach to the major issues as both naïve and simplistic, both his domestic and world views were based on his life's experience, careful examination and understanding of the issues, and a strong dose of old-fashioned, practical wisdom.

Reagan's first challenge as commander in chief was to formulate an effective economic policy, one in which the budget would be balanced; federal spending caused by President Carter's social welfare programs reduced; tax cuts implemented; and economic growth stimulated. Defense spending would be increased considerably, however, in order to restore the morale and effectiveness of the military, which had eroded during the Carter era.

Reagan's controversial adherence to "supply side" economic theory was vigorously attacked by Democrats and even by some in his own administration, including the budget director, David Stockman. Most importantly, however, Reagan, following the policy of his predecessors—his successors would do likewise—was careful not to reduce Social Security benefits. While he succeeded in pushing his economic program through the Congress, by the fall of 1982, the nation had fallen into its worst recession since the early thirties.

Meanwhile, Reagan had to survive, literally, the greatest challenge of his first term. On the early afternoon of March 30, 1981, two months and ten days into his presidency, Reagan, who had just concluded an address before the Construction Trades Council at the Washington Hilton, was emerging

from the hotel's ballroom entrance and was moving toward the presidential limousine when a young man approached and began to fire at the presidential entourage. Members of Reagan's Secret Service detail shoved him into the limousine (photos at right).

The president's assailant, John Hinckley Jr., whose motive in firing at Reagan would later be revealed as a pathetic attempt to impress the film actress Jodie Foster, came from an affluent Denver family. Hinckley's fire had apparently wounded only the president's press secretary, James Brady, a Secret Service man and a District of Columbia police officer, all of whom lay sprawled on the ground. It was originally announced that Brady, bleeding profusely from a head wound, was dead. He survived, however, as did the other wounded men.

As the limousine driver raced off toward the White House, it became apparent that Reagan, too, had been wounded, and that he had sustained a serious injury. Reversing course, the driver sped to the George Washington University Hospital. There, in the Emergency Room, as doctors tore off the president's clothing, they discovered that he had suffered a serious gunshot wound to the chest. One of the would-be assassin's bullets, after ricocheting off the limousine, had entered the president's body under his left arm. From there, the bullet had smashed into his rib and then coursed through his chest, coming to rest in his left lung, barely an inch from his heart.

Meanwhile, Nancy had just returned to the White House from a function and was meeting in the solarium with the head usher of the Executive Mansion and her decorator when the head of her Secret Service detail came into the room and told her of the shooting, assuring her that the president hadn't been hit, but that he had been taken to the hospital with the wounded men. Hearing the word "shooting," Nancy insisted on going there immediately, however, and she would soon learn that her beloved Ronnie had in fact been wounded.

As the president was being prepared for surgery, glancing up at one of the physicians who would operate, he quipped, "I hope you're a Republican." Despite Reagan's good humor and grace under pressure, he had been gravely wounded and could have died while under the knife. His surgeons removed a Devastator bullet from his lung, which had filled with blood, making it extremely difficult

and painful for him to breathe. Then, within twenty-four hours, he developed a staph infection. On his return to the White House, reflecting on his close call, the president wrote in his diary, "Whatever happens now, I owe my life to God and will try to serve him every way I can."

As the president lay on the operating table undergoing the surgery his physicians hoped would save his life, a serious dispute was erupting in the White House. Several of his key aides were meeting to discuss whether or not to invoke provisions of the Twenty-Fifth Amendment to the Constitution dealing with the issue of succession in the event that the president is incapacitated. As the group deliberated, they were very much aware that the media and, indeed, others throughout the United States who had heard the first, alarming news bulletins, were wondering: Who is now running the country?

That question's implications were of crucial importance, as one of the president's responsibilities is to determine how to respond in the event of a nuclear attack. To complicate matters, Vice President Bush was at that time airborne, on his way to a speaking engagement in Texas.

As the discussion continued, one of the participants, Secretary of State Alexander M. Haig Jr., left the meeting. Dashing into the White House Press Room, perspiring and out of breath, he blurted out, "I'm in charge," not only shocking his colleagues—his outburst would lead eventually to his departure from the administration—but betraying his gross ignorance of the constitutionally mandated order of succession, in which the secretary of state is only the fourth in line of presidential succession. In any event, the provisions of the Twenty-Fifth Amendment pertaining to the president's incapacity were not invoked.

As Reagan, back in the White House in a matter of days, gradually resumed his usual schedule, he took two unprecedented actions. In the first instance, he took an implacable stand when con-

fronted with a national crisis. The air controllers' union, PATCO, had called a strike, one that threatened to cripple the nation's air transportation system. On August 3, Reagan gave the controllers forty-eight hours to return to work or be fired. True to his word, the president dismissed scores of those who refused to comply with his order. In the second instance, the following month, the president appointed Sandra Day O'Connor as the first woman to serve on the U.S. Supreme Court.

Foreign affairs issues would largely occupy the president in the remaining years of his first term. In June 1982, the Israeli Defense Forces, in an effort to quell attacks against Israeli citizens by the Palestine Liberation Organization [PLO], and acting in response to an attack in London against Israel's ambassador to the United Kingdom, Shlomo Argov, launched an incursion into southern Lebanon, the seat of the PLO's Kingdom of Terror. Israel's involvement in the civil war that had raged for almost a decade between Lebanon's Christian and Muslim populations resulted in the PLO's banishment to Tunis. Ongoing tensions among Lebanon's various religious factions, however, would lead the Reagan administration to send a detachment of Marines to Beirut to serve as peacekeepers, an action that proved deadly when, on October 23, 1983, 241 Marines were killed as a suicide bomber rammed an explosives-laden car into their barracks.

Two days later, almost halfway around the world, a 1700-man force of U.S. Marines and Army Rangers landed on Grenada, a miniscule Caribbean island whose Marxist, Castro-friendly government had allowed the Soviets to construct a major airfield outside the capital, St. Georges. The immediate reasons for the invasion, carried out at the behest of the Organization of Eastern Caribbean States [OECS] and dubbed "Operation Urgent Fury," included the instability of Grenada's government following the assassination of its prime minister, Maurice Bishop, and concern for the safety of the scores of American students then enrolled at the island's medical school.

While the U.S. forces easily took control of the island, despite the use of antiquated Esso road maps—leading to the election of a democratic government—Reagan's critics viewed the episode as an attempt to deflect attention from the worsening situation in Lebanon. Reagan's detractors also expressed concern over the rupture in U.S.-British relations stemming from the failure of the administration to inform the prime minister, Margaret Thatcher—she was one of the president's most ardent political allies—of its intention to invade a member-nation of the British Commonwealth. Years later, it would be revealed that while the administration had in fact sent a message by fax to the prime minister, the wrong number had been used, and that the fax had gone instead to a plastics factory in Ipswich. Someone at the factory, realizing that a mistake had been made, contacted the Foreign Office in London, only to be told to put the fax in the mail.

The invasion of Grenada was also meant to send a signal to Nicaragua's Sandinistas, whose activities were of growing concern to U.S. policy makers, that just as Reagan, who in May 1984 described the group as being communists, had the will to send troops to the Caribbean, he could also launch operations in Latin America. Then in May 1984, Reagan called for aid to the opposition, known as contras.

The president's views were not wholly shared with the Congress, which on October 10, 1984, passed the Second Boland Amendment, barring the solicitation of third party countries in support of the contras. A provision of that legislation also forbade U.S. intelligence and defense agencies from using funds available to them for military or political operations in Nicaragua.

There was yet another message in the U.S. invasion of Grenada, which was directed at the Soviet Union. By having launched that military operation, Reagan wanted the Soviets to understand that he would not tolerate outside intervention in the Western Hemisphere. U.S.-Soviet relations, having already been damaged during the Carter presidency due to the Soviet invasion of Afghanistan, were further strained when on September 1, 1983, a Soviet fighter plane downed Korean Airlines flight 007 as it drifted off course near the Pacific coast of Russia. That seemingly unnecessary attack, which claimed the lives of all 259 onboard, served to harden public opinion in the United States, causing many Americans to agree with Reagan's assessment, made earlier that year during an address to the National Association of Evangelicals, that the Soviet Union was an "evil empire."

During the early years of his administration, Reagan had combined harsh rhetoric with calls for renewed discussion of arms control issues. In January 1984, the president suggested that the U.S. and the Soviet Union enter into nuclear arms talks in Geneva and Vienna. Having carefully explored the issue of nuclear armament for nearly two decades, he had come to oppose the doctrine of Mutually Assured Destruction [MAD], a principle both superpowers had subscribed to throughout most of the cold war, their rationale being that as both nations possessed huge stores of deadly nuclear weapons, neither one would launch an attack.

Reagan, fearing that the Biblical prophecy regarding Armageddon would one day be fulfilled in a nuclear confrontation, advocated the abolition of all nuclear weapons. He was realistic enough, however, to realize that such an all-encompassing ban would not likely occur as long as the cold war continued. Thus he formulated a plan for the defense of the United States against nuclear attack. It was based on information he had gathered fifteen years earlier, during his visit while governor of California to the Lawrence Livermore Laboratory in the company of Dr. Edward Teller. Convinced that the U.S. would never launch a first strike, the president reasoned that if a system could be developed to shoot down incoming missiles before they could reach their target, the value of offensive missiles to the other side would be seriously compromised.

While realizing that his ideas concerning missile defense were highly controversial, Reagan on March 23, 1983, against the advice of some of his closest advisers, informed a nationwide television audience that he planned to establish a new program, one that would run counter to the conventional wisdom of MAD. The president proposed that a Strategic Defense Initiative [SDI] be launched. To make his point, addressing a question to the American people, he asked, "What if free people could live secure in the knowledge that their security did not rest upon the threat of instant U.S. retaliation to deter a Soviet attack, that we could intercept and destroy strategic ballistic missiles before they reached our own soil or that of our allies?"

Reagan's proposal, dubbed derisively as "Star Wars" by his critics both in Congress and in the media, was the president's courageous attempt to end the nuclear stalemate that had bedeviled U.S.-Soviet relations throughout much of the cold war. In advocating SDI, he knew that it might take many years, as well as a huge expenditure of funds, to develop an effective missile defense system. The president nevertheless had the vision to begin the process. He was convinced that American ingenuity, coupled with rapid advances in technology, would eventually prevail. During Reagan's second term, his faith in SDI would reap major dividends in U.S.-Soviet relations.

As the summer of 1984 approached, no one doubted that Reagan would seek a second term. Some Republicans, however, questioned whether, given his age—he was the oldest person in American history to have become president—and his health, having survived serious injury in the attempt on his life, he would have the stamina to fulfill the enormous responsibilities of a second four-year term.

At the 1984 Republican National Convention in Dallas, where Reagan was nominated by acclamation, he put forth the theme of "Morning in America"—that now is the time for the nation and its citizenry to reclaim past glory through both optimism and honest endeavor. Reagan's opponent, Walter Mondale, a seasoned politician, had served as a U.S. senator from Minnesota and as Jimmy Carter's vice president. Mondale chose as his running mate a member of Congress from New York, Geraldine Ferraro. She will go down in American history as the first woman to run for national office.

When Reagan and Mondale met in Louisville, Kentucky, on October 7 for their debate on domestic issues, the president, who had been over-prepared by his staff with facts and figures, stumbled and stammered. His lackluster performance appeared to confirm fears that Reagan was simply too old to effectively govern the nation. In the two week interim between his debacle in Louisville and the second and final debate in Kansas City, Reagan refrained from engaging in skull sessions and mock debates, to excellent advantage, as he recovered his equilibrium.

While focusing during the debate on foreign affairs, the panel did touch, inevitably, on the issue of Reagan's age. One of Reagan's questioners, asking whether his age would be a factor, even a handicap, during the campaign, elicited an unexpected response from the president, "I'm not going to exploit for political purposes my opponent's youth and inexperience," he said in the gentle, humor-inflected tone he so often used to great advantage. He had done it again. The national television audience was electrified.

On November 4, 1984, President Reagan was reelected in a landslide, winning in forty-nine states and garnering fifty-nine percent of the popular vote. As he looked forward to his second term, he was confident that he would bring prosperity to the American people and achieve progress in relations with the Soviet Union. As he recovered from the rigors of the campaign, Reagan could not know that severe personal and political trials would mark the four years ahead.

Chapter Eight
The President's
Second Term

The president began his new term by shaking up his senior staff. James Baker, seemingly restless as chief of staff, became Reagan's treasury secretary, shifting jobs with former Wall Street executive Donald Regan, while the ever-loyal Edwin Meese moved to the Justice Department as attorney general. Although those changes were regarded at the time as typical of the personnel-jockeying that often characterizes the beginning of a presidential term, they would have major repercussions as the Iran-contra crisis unfolded.

The new administration was barely settling in when a major development occurred. On March 11, 1985, the president was awakened at 4:00 a.m. with the news that the Soviet leader, Konstantin Chernenko, had died in Moscow. Chernenko, who had replaced the hard-line former KGB head, Yuri Andropov, only the previous year, and who in his brief term had made tentative moves toward reform, was succeeded by a high-level bureaucrat, fifty-four-year-old Mikhail Gorbachev.

Reagan sent Vice President Bush and Secretary of State George Shultz—the latter had replaced Haig in 1982—to represent him at Chernenko's funeral. Bush was carrying a letter from the president inviting Gorbachev to attend a summit meeting in the United States. Two weeks later, replying, the new Soviet general secretary expressed his willingness to do so, but wanted to meet outside the U.S.

Gorbachev had come to power at the moment when fissures were beginning to appear in the Soviet

structure. That vast nation, encompassing nine time zones, as well as diverse ethnic groups, was spending enormous amounts of money on armaments and defense while continuing to rule a satellite empire extending across Central and Eastern Europe. Reagan and his associates knew relatively little about Gorbachev; they were aware, however, that the British Prime Minister, Margaret Thatcher, had spent a day with him the previous December, during Gorbachev's visit to London as part of a delegation of high-ranking Soviet officials. Prime Minister Thatcher had come away from that meeting claiming, "We can do business with him."

In February 1986, addressing the Twenty-Seventh Congress of the Communist Party of the Soviet Union, the new general secretary startled the world by calling for "glasnost," which translates as "openness," and "perestroika," the Russian word for "restructuring." As specialists in the administration on the Soviet Union agonized over Gorbachev's true intentions, President Reagan, ever the realistic optimist, saw the potential for the betterment of U.S.-Soviet relations.

That improvement in relations began in Geneva, where, on the morning of November 19, 1986, the President of the United States greeted the leader of the Soviet Union on the steps of the Villa Fleur d'Eau. As Gorbachev, attired in a heavy topcoat and hat, got out of his official car, Reagan, twenty years his senior, and despite the chill in the air both coatless and hatless, bounded down the steps, the picture of health and vigor. During their first meeting, scheduled to last fifteen minutes but going on for more than an hour, the two men, alone save for their respective translators, established an almost immediate rapport that would stand them in good stead in the difficult negotiations that lay ahead.

That afternoon, as both U.S. and Soviet experts on arms control made their presentations, Reagan suggested to Gorbachev that they adjourn to a nearby cottage for another private conversation.

He agreed. Then, as the leaders of the world's two superpowers sat facing each other in comfortable armchairs beside a roaring fire, they debated the Strategic Defense Initiative [SDI]. Reagan insisted that SDI was defensive in nature and thus permitted under the ABM treaty that had been signed by the U.S. and the Soviet Union during the past decade. In urging that they come to an agreement concerning nuclear arms control, Reagan stated, "You must know it's an arms race you can't win, because we are not going to allow you to maintain this superiority over us." The president's bold language notwithstanding, Gorbachev accepted Reagan's invitation to participate in a future summit in Washington and the secretary general invited the president to one in Moscow. Reagan left Geneva confident that although Gorbachev was a tough-minded true-believer in the Soviet system he was, nevertheless, a man with whom he could talk.

Over the next few months, the two leaders would exchange substantive letters, some of them hand-written, in preparation for their Washington meeting. Then, in July 1986, Reagan was given new evidence of Soviet capriciousness when Nicholas Daniloff, a Moscow correspondent for *U.S. News & World Report*, was arrested and charged with spying for the United States. While the Daniloff affair strained Reagan's relationship with Gorbachev, the situation eased somewhat with the correspondent's release in exchange for the return to the Soviets of Gennadi Zakharov, one of their "diplomats" who had been charged by the U.S. with espionage.

As the Daniloff issue was winding down, Gorbachev surprised Reagan by suggesting an impromptu summit—it would be dubbed by the media a "non-summit"—to be held either in a major Western European capital or in Iceland. The president, wary of Soviet intentions, opted for a two-day meeting in the latter, more remote, setting. Their "non-summit" took place in the capital, Reykjavik, on October 11 and 12. All sessions were held at Hofdi House, a small, isolated

building located on the city's waterfront.

The agenda centered on arms control, with secondary, but important, focus placed on human rights issues. The plight of Soviet Jews, many of them designated as refuseniks or as prisoners of conscience, was very much on Reagan's mind as he confronted Gorbachev. While the Soviet Union had advanced beyond the excesses of the Stalin era, state-sponsored anti-Semitism still existed and many Jews who desired to be repatriated to Israel or to be allowed to live in the West were being denied their basic right of free emigration—one that the U.S.S.R. has recognized as a signatory to the Universal Declaration of Human Rights and other international agreements. To make matters worse, while the fierce brutality of the Stalin era had somewhat lessened, there still existed a gulag in which thousands of human rights campaigners, including Jewish refuseniks and prisoners of conscience, among other dissidents, were imprisoned in horrendous conditions.

While the leaders and their aides met, the two thousand correspondents working in the International Press Center were doing so under a total news blackout. With little to report on, they spent a lot of time interviewing one another, sampling local delicacies that had been put on display there by promotionally savvy food distributors, and competing in a raffle for an all-expenses-paid vacation in Iceland. The winner, a Japanese journalist, provoked practically the only laughter of the entire summit among his bored colleagues when he refused, at first, to kiss the reigning Miss Iceland, which was required in order that he receive his prize. He eventually succumbed to the hoots and whistles of his fellow correspondents.

At Hofdi House, however, there was little levity as Reagan and Gorbachev faced off over SDI. In his memoir, Reagan would describe the second and final day at Reykjavik as "one of the longest, most disappointing, and ultimately, angriest days of my presidency." After working through the night, the U.S. and Soviet teams had made significant progress on the issues of nuclear missiles, other nuclear weapons, and verification procedures. Things appeared to be going so smoothly that Reagan and Gorbachev continued to talk beyond the summit's announced noon deadline. By evening, Reagan was convinced that he and his advisers had negotiated the most far-reaching weapons reductions since the onset of the cold war.

Then, quite unexpectedly, Gorbachev insisted that all that had been agreed upon would hinge on whether the U.S. would relinquish SDI. Reagan, who knew that the Soviets were at work on their own missile defense system, refused to grant such a concession; it was simply too dangerous. He did, however, offer to share the system with the Soviet Union, as well as with other nations, once it was deployable. The Soviet general secretary, either not comprehending or quite believing Reagan's promise, held firm: The U.S. must give up SDI or the agreements reached at Reykjavik would be rendered null

Reagan gives his weekly radio address, November 9, 1985, at the Voice of America *studio in Washington. The address was beamed by the* Voice of America *to the Soviet Union.*

and void. Stung by Gorbachev's last-minute about-face, the president, turning to Secretary of State Shultz, said, "Let's go; we're leaving."

That evening, a media-driven firestorm of criticism came down upon the president. As Reagan flew across the Atlantic Ocean toward Washington, his political opponents, both at home and in Europe, expressed their anger at his having left the summit without accepting the arms reduction agreements that had been agreed to by Gorbachev. In an eerie reprise of the denigrating comments concerning his intelligence, judgment, and leadership capability that had dogged his early political career, the president was now being unmercifully pilloried.

Reagan was convinced, however, that his action had been the correct one. He often sought advice from people outside the administration, including the author Susan Massie, who had observed the inner workings of the Soviet system, and the president understood that the Soviet Union was in the throes of a severe fiscal crisis and thus simply could not then or in the long run hope to keep pace with the U.S. regarding defense spending.

In his dealings with the Soviet Union up to that point, the president had chosen a path different from those of his immediate predecessors: there had not been, nor would there be, anything like the "Spirit of Glassboro" at the conclusion of the meeting in June 1967 between President Lyndon Johnson and his Soviet counterpart, Alexei Kosygin. Nor would there be continuation of the détente with the Soviet Union that had been engineered by President Nixon and his secretary of state, Henry Kissinger, during summits with Leonid Brezhnev. Nor would Reagan engage in photo ops, as Gerald Ford had done when he had rushed off to Vladivostok to have his picture taken with Brezhnev. And Reagan would certainly not show any sign of weakness, as Carter had exhibited in response to Soviet aggression.

And it is difficult to imagine any of Reagan's predecessors standing before the Berlin Wall—as the president would do on June 6, 1987—demanding of

Gorbachev that he tear down that quintessential symbol of the Soviet Union's aggressive cold war policy. Similarly, it would be hard to imagine Johnson, Nixon, Ford, or Carter entertaining refuseniks and other dissidents at the American Embassy in Moscow during a tense summit meeting with the Soviet leader. But that is exactly what President Reagan would have the sheer guts to do on the evening of May 30, 1988. The following afternoon, the president would tell the student body at Moscow State University, "In this Moscow spring, this May 1988, we may be allowed that hope, that freedom like the fresh green sapling planted over Tolstoy's grave, will blossom forth at last in the rich fertile soil of your people and culture."

As he departed from Reykjavik in the late afternoon on October 12, 1986, the president was more determined than ever in his goal to weaken the Soviet Union economically, thus bringing on the implosion of its entire system. While the better part of the year following that summit would be marked by tensions over SDI, Gorbachev did travel to Washington in late 1987 for a meeting with the president, resulting in the signing of the landmark INF Treaty in which four percent of each side's nuclear weapons would be eliminated. On December 6, the day before the first session of the summit, more than 200,000 Americans of all faiths gathered at the Mall in Washington to participate in Freedom Sunday for Soviet Jewry. That expression of support for human rights was addressed by major political figures, including Vice President Bush and a future vice president, Al Gore, as well as by recently released Jewish dissidents, including former Soviet prisoner of conscience Natan Sharansky. If he hadn't gotten the message before December 6, 1988, Gorbachev now had dramatic proof of America's determination to demand the compliance of his government with its international obligations.

While Reagan would during his second term devote a considerable amount of time to dealing with the Soviets, he would also confront serious personal and national issues. In July 1985 he underwent colon cancer surgery, making a speedy recovery. Then on October 2, he and Nancy's close friend, the film star Rock Hudson, died of AIDS. His death energized the president into making a strong commitment to fighting the disease, which would soon become a pandemic. The surgeon general, Dr. C. Everett Koop, a well respected physician and academician who had long advocated taking action, led the fight against AIDS, while the president created a special commission charged with discovering and evaluating potential treatments and preventatives.

In the late winter of 1986, the Reagans attended the memorial service for the victims of the Challenger disaster. The space craft had exploded just seventy-three seconds after takeoff, killing all those on board, including Christa McAuliffe, a school teacher from New Hampshire. The loss of the Challenger called attention to systemic failings of the National Aeronautics and Space Administration [NASA]—failings that in a way prefigured the catastrophic loss in 2003 of the Columbia space shuttle.

While much of Reagan's attention in 1986 centered on the Soviet Union, Central America, and the Middle East, he also had cause for concern over developments in the southern Mediterranean, where the Libyan dictator, Muammar al-Qaddafi, already suspected of terrorist intentions against the president, was threatening the operations of the U.S. Sixth Fleet. In late March, an American serviceman was killed in the bombing of a Berlin nightclub frequented by G.I.'s in a terrorist act attributed by U.S. intelligence to Libya. Following consultation with his military advisers, as well as with Prime Minister Thatcher, President Reagan decided to attack the center, located within Qaddafi's military headquarters and barracks, housing Libya's intelligence apparatus.

Late on the night of April 14, following a briefing for the Congressional leadership, American warplanes appeared over Tripoli. During the

eleven-minute attack, several civilians, including Qaddafi's adopted daughter, were killed when some of the bombs missed the intended target. Reagan's action was widely praised: seventy per cent of the thousands who sent messages to the White House approved the raid. While the bombing did inhibit Libyan-sponsored terrorism for a time, on December 21, 1988, in the waning days of the Reagan administration, Pan American Airways' flight 103, bound from Heathrow Airport near London to New York, was blown out of the sky over Lockerbee, Scotland. It would later be determined that Libyan terrorists had orchestrated and carried out the heinous action.

All of those issues would pale in importance to the crisis brought about on November 2, 1986, with the publication by Al-Shiraa, a relatively obscure Lebanese newspaper, of an article in which it was claimed that the United States had been selling arms to Iran. That claim, verified the following day by the Iranian government, led to the unraveling of the scandal that would come to be known as the Iran-contra affair. The scandal's background is complex: Not all of the facts concerning its inception are as yet public knowledge, owing both to the conflicting accounts of some of the key players and the continued classification on national security grounds of a number of pertinent documents.

In examining and evaluating Iran-contra's causes and progression, the Watergate scandal of the Nixon era comes to mind. It is difficult, even now, to piece together a totally cogent account of the primary cause of Iran-contra, which seriously diminished Reagan's standing with the American people and nearly led to his impeachment. We do know that the president, a warm-hearted and compassionate man, was deeply troubled that as he began his second term, six Americans were being held hostage in Lebanon by terrorist cells affiliated with the fanatic Islamic Jihad [Party of God] organization. The taking of the hostages, the earlier bombing of the Marine Barracks in Beirut, and other acts of terror against U.S. interests in

Lebanon were jeopardizing the Reagan administration's goal of achieving stability there, as well as a comprehensive agreement between the Israelis and the Palestinians.

It was increasingly clear to the Reagan administration that Iran was behind the bombings and hostage-takings. Indeed, early in 1984, after terrorists had murdered Malcolm Kerr, the president of the American University in Beirut, the president had publicly denounced the Khomeini regime. The previous December, the State Department had initiated Operation Staunch, an effort to discourage other nations from selling arms to Iran, which was then engaged in a bloody war with its neighbor, Iraq.

U.S. hostility toward Iran increased when on June 14, 1985, terrorists associated with Islamic Jihad hijacked TWA flight 847 as it left Athens. Following the aircraft's arrival in Beirut, one of the passengers, Navy diver Robert Stethem, was murdered and his body thrown onto the tarmac. The hijacking and, to a strong degree, the kidnapping of Americans in Lebanon, was connected to the fate of seventeen imprisoned members of Al-Da'wa al-Islamia, a Shiite political group with headquarters in Tehran. The Al-Dawa prisoners had been held in Kuwait since just after the bombing in December 1983 of the U.S. and French embassies there. The Iranian-backed terrorists— the brother- in-law of one of them was the head of Islamic Jihad—would figure prominently in the negotiations for the release of the TWA passengers and crew, as well as in later discussions concerning the fate of the U.S. hostages being held in Lebanon.

While the president and his senior cabinet officers, Secretary of State Shultz and Secretary of Defense Caspar Weinberger, sought to identify Iran as a pariah state and weaken it in its conflict with Iraq, other members of the administration sought a new opening to the nation that under the Shah had been one of America's closest allies. Those officials, working mainly in the National

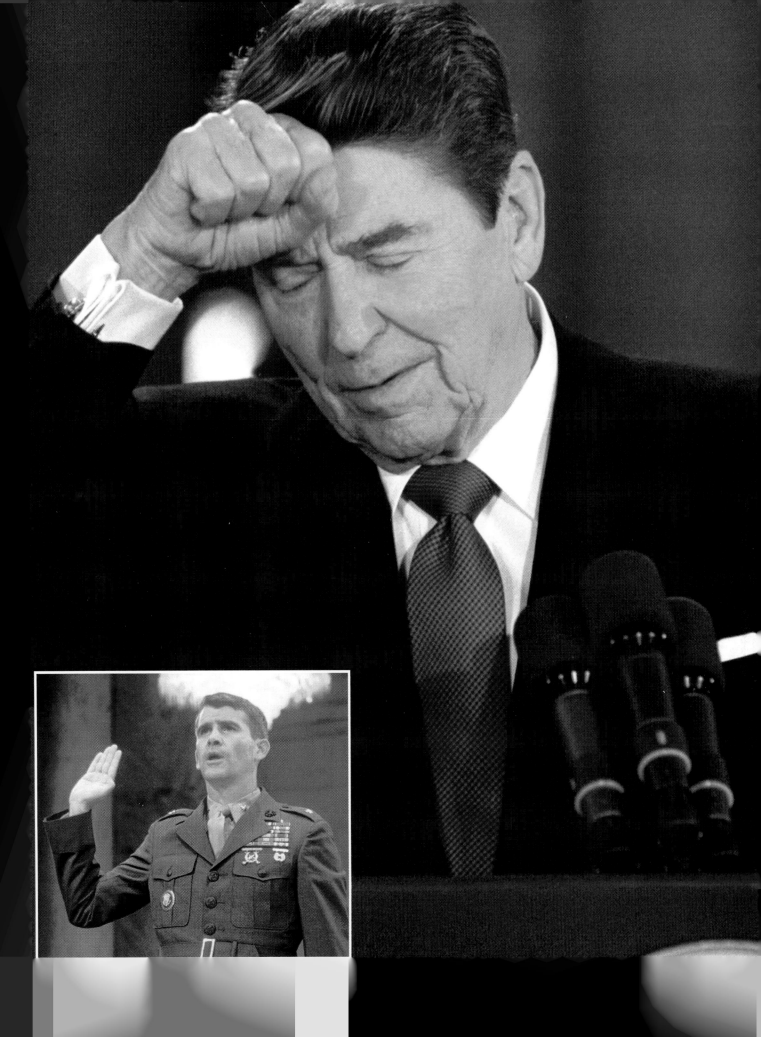

Security Council and supported by the influential director of central intelligence, William Casey, believed that given Iran's strategic location, with frontage on both the Persian Gulf and on the Caspian Sea facing the Soviet Union, its substantial oil reserves, large population, and considerable land mass, it was imperative for United States to renew its relationship with Iran—the menacing and virulently anti-Western Khomeini notwithstanding.

In October 1984, based on the conclusions of an interagency study authorized by Robert McFarlane, the national security adviser, in anticipation of the elderly Khomeini's death, it was suggested that even after the Iranian cleric's demise, the U.S. would have little influence in Iran. McFarlane, however, continued to press for an opening to the Iranians and was supported in a memorandum written by Graham Fuller, the CIA's intelligence officer for the Near East and South Asia. In his May 1985 memo, Fuller expressed his view that the Khomeini regime was faltering. In the anticipated struggle for succession, he wrote, "The US has almost no cards to play; the USSR has many."

As the NSC and the CIA studied the possibility of rapprochement with Iran—one that might have the additional benefit of enhancing the possibility of the release of some or all of the American hostages—Manucher Ghorbanifar, a shadowy Iranian national, arms merchant, and sometime CIA informant, told a former CIA officer, as well as high-level officials in Israel, that the Iranian government, desperate for new weaponry and spare parts in order to continue its war against Iraq, might be willing to release the hostages in return for arms. During his meetings in Israel and later in Washington, Ghorbanifar was convincing, claiming that certain "moderates" in the Iranian government would be strengthened if they could obtain weapons to be used against Iraq. Further, upon Khomeini's death, the moderates would express their gratitude by bringing Iran into a pro-Western stance.

Israel was to play a major role initially in the arms shipments, transferring TOW anti-tank missiles to Iran and having its own stocks replenished by the United States. McFarlane presented the plan to the president in July 1985 as he recuperated from his colon cancer surgery. Reagan in turn discussed the scheme with his top advisers on August 6 during a meeting in the White House. Approving the plan, he telephoned McFarlane several days later with his sign-off.

In agreeing to the arms sales to Iran, Reagan was motivated primarily by concern for the hostages' welfare. He knew, through having viewed videotaped evidence, that William Buckley had been tortured by his captors. Thus the president assumed that the other hostages were being subjected to physical abuse. In addition, Reagan, against the advice of some of his closest advisers, had engaged in emotionally-wrenching meetings with several of the hostages' families. The president was also aware of the publicity campaign then being conducted by Peggy Say on behalf of her brother, Terry Anderson, the Middle East bureau chief of the Associated Press, who had been kidnapped on March 16, 1985.

To Reagan's way of thinking, he was not dealing directly with the terrorists who had actually taken the Americans hostage. Rather, he believed that the beneficiaries of the arms sales in Iran could influence the hostage-takers. As he explained to key members of his staff, "It's the same thing as if one of my children was kidnapped and there was a demand for ransom. Sure, I don't believe in ransom because it leads to more kidnapping. But if I find out there's somebody who has access to the kidnapper and can get my child back without doing anything for the kidnapper, I'd sure do that," Reagan continued. "And it would be perfectly fitting for me to reward that individual if he got my child back. That's not paying ransom to the kidnappers."

On August 19, the Israelis, with the participation of well-connected private citizens and with bridge

funding provided by Saudi financier Adnan Khashoggi, shipped 96 TOW missiles to Iran. While no hostages were released following that initial shipment, following a further shipment, of 408 TOW's, in mid-September, the Rev. Benjamin Weir, a Presbyterian missionary who had been kidnapped on May 8, 1984, was released.

Then, in late October, the Iranians raised the ante, demanding a quantity of HAWK missiles in exchange for the further release of hostages. In late November, the missiles were sent. When the packages were opened, however, the Iranians discovered that the missiles bore Israeli markings. Making matters even worse, the missiles were not capable of shooting down high-flying Iraqi aircraft. That snafu led the Reagan administration to a fateful decision: the U.S. would now take over the arms shipments, cutting out the Israeli middlemen. Assigned the responsibility of coordinating the sales was Oliver North, a Marine lieutenant colonel and Vietnam combat veteran who was serving as the NSC's director of politico-military affairs. As North moved to the center of the administration's dealings with Iran, he continued to play a major role in seeking non-governmental funding for the Nicaraguan contras. How a relatively junior-level field grade officer, working out of an office in the basement of the White House, was able to aggrandize such immense power remains one of Iran-contra's major mysteries.

In order to conduct the arms sales, North, who had proven his adeptness at working his way through the maze of Washington's political and military bureaucracies, created "The Enterprise," a network of dummy corporations and foreign bank accounts, administered by Richard Secord, a retired Air Forced Major General, and Albert Hakim, an expatriate Iranian businessman living in California. As the Reagan biographer Lou Cannon noted, the Enterprise would realize nearly $48 million from the sales—the Iranians were grossly overcharged for their purchases—as well as from the contributions of private donors and third-party countries, eventually expending more

than $38 million dollars on covert activities, including the diversion of $3.8 million to the contras.

The revelation of the arms sales sent the administration into free fall. Within days of the disclosure, and following a disastrous press conference during which the president had provided incomplete information, a first attempt was made at damage control: Attorney General Meese was appointed to launch an internal investigation. North, on learning that Meese's aides intended to examine his files, began to shred documents. While a considerable amount of material was destroyed, Meese's people discovered one item that had somehow escaped obliteration, a memorandum that had been written on April 4 of that year by North—one that would have even more ominous ramifications for Reagan's presidency— spelling out details of the diversion of funds from the arms sales to the contras.

Whatever North's true motivation was, he did know that the president was totally committed to the contras. Reagan was certain that if the Sandinistas were to prevail, their form of Marxist rule would inevitably be exported throughout Central America. As early as December 1981, the president had authorized the CIA to conduct a covert action program to "support and conduct...paramilitary operations against...Nicaragua." The president had also asked the State Department to establish an Office of Public Diplomacy for Latin America, which would develop popular support for the contras, as well as raise funds for the furtherance of their cause.

North had been present at numerous White House meetings during which the president and members of the administration had asked private citizens to contribute funds in support of the contras' effort. It is possible then to conclude that when North arranged for the diversion of some of the profits from the arms sales to Iran, he believed that he was acting in accordance with the president's wish. If that was his intention, however, he

was mistaken, for in all of the voluminous documentary material concerning Iran-contra, no direct order has ever been discovered linking Reagan to the diversion.

The record clearly indicates that although the president was engaged in an ongoing battle with Congress to achieve support for the contras, he constantly stressed that everything done in their support must be accomplished by legal means. He knew that the Sandinista government and its fellow travelers in the United States were engaged in a major disinformation campaign aimed at hiding both the true nature of the regime and its aggressive intentions against neighboring nations.

In his memoir, Reagan acknowledged that North and other key members of the administration involved in assisting the contras knew of his own deep-felt identification with their struggle, as well as of his frustration in not being able to convince Congress of the importance of the contras' survival. At the same time, however, he told his staff, "We can't break the law."

Revelation of the diversion resulted in North's firing and, most importantly, the appointment by President Reagan of a special review board chaired by a former senator, John Tower of Texas. In mid-December, Congress established a special joint committee to examine the affair. Then on December 17, a three-judge panel of the U.S. Court of Appeals appointed Lawrence Walsh, a former federal judge, as independent counsel. Lastly, on Christmas Eve, the president, in his second attempt at damage control, called home his ambassador to NATO, David Abshire, a highly respected scholar, to serve as special adviser on the Iran-contra affair.

The following February, the Tower Commission released its report, blaming the president for failing to ensure the proper functioning of the National Security Council. In November 1987, the joint Congressional Committee in its report—with dissent from its Republican minority members—criticized North, McFarlane, his successor, Admiral John Poindexter, and, posthumously, William Casey who had died on May 6, concluding that the ultimate responsibility for the Iran-contra affair lay with the president. Walsh, who sought indictments at the cabinet and likely the vice presidential and presidential levels—he did indict Weinberger—had to be content with the convictions and/or guilty pleas of Hakim, McFarlane, North, Poindexter, Secord and other lesser players. North's and Poindexter's convictions would be overturned, while others, as well as Weinberger's indictment, would be voided on December 24, 1992, the day President George Hebert Walker Bush granted them pardons.

While President Reagan had the best of intentions in his passionate desire to free the hostages, sadly, while additional ones would be freed, the arms sales had the very much undesired effect of encouraging additional kidnappings because the U.S. had revealed its major weak spot—its willingness to negotiate with terrorists and to continue to provide them with arms. As Reagan's associates continued to meet with Iranian representatives in the late summer and early fall of 1986, three additional Americans were taken hostage in the revolving door atmosphere that had come to exist.

The president had constantly stressed his support for the contras, but it is very unlikely that he would have approved of North's scheme for the diversion of funds. While his reputation would suffer due to Iran-contra—his approval rating would temporarily nosedive—he would achieve an impressive comeback, one that would enable him to engage the Soviets during the remaining months of his last term. Faced with the issue of whether or not to believe Reagan's assertion that he did not have prior knowledge of the diversion of funds to the contras, and in the absence of documents proving otherwise, the American people, for the most part, have accepted Reagan's word.

Chapter Nine
"My Fellow Americans…"

President Reagan was nearly 78 years old when he left office on January 20, 1989, but hardly looked his age. With his ruddy complexion, still jet-black hair, and firm body—toned by horseback riding and log-splitting at his and Nancy's beloved retreat, Rancho del Cielo—Ron had slowed down a bit, but he still looked, and acted, years younger.

Then one day, while horseback riding during a visit to Mexico, the president was thrown to the ground and suffered a head injury. On examination, while he was found to be suffering from the early stages of Alzheimer's disease, despite the devastating diagnosis, he was found to have a high I.Q.

Had there been signs of Alzheimer's much earlier—signs that the president's loved ones and associates had overlooked? Dr. C. Everett Koop, the Reagan administration's surgeon general, never saw any signs of the disease during Reagan's Oval Office years. The first time the public became painfully aware of the president's decline was during a birthday party for the visiting British prime minister, Margaret Thatcher, which took place at the then recently-opened Ronald Reagan Museum and Library, in Simi Valley, California. On that occasion, the president was to introduce the prime minister. Clutching the three-by-five index cards he always used when addressing an audience, the president made his introduction, to warm applause. Then, as he attempted to shift to the next card in order to make further remarks, he could not move it and repeated what he had just said. His friendly audience applauded once again, but it was

He could have summoned an aide to draft a statement to be delivered to the media. But that was not Ronald Reagan's style. The great communicator believed that it was his duty to communicate this news himself.

Thus, on November 5, 1994, in a gesture of grace and courage so typical of him—his action would be emulated in June 2003 by Kennedy brother-in-law, administration official, and 1972 vice presidential candidate R. Sargent Shriver in a letter to the *Washington Post* disclosing that he was in the early stages of the disease—the now eighty-three-year-old former president, in a hand-written note to the people he had so enthusiastically served for two terms, told them what the future held in store.

My Fellow Americans,

I have recently been told that I am one of the millions of Americans who will be afflicted with Alzheimer's disease.

Upon learning this news, Nancy and I had to decide whether as private citizens we would keep this a private matter or whether we would make this news known in a public way.

In the past Nancy suffered from breast cancer and I had my cancer surgeries. We found that through our open disclosures we were able to raise public awareness. We were happy that as a result many more people underwent testing.

They were treated in early stages and able to return to normal, healthy lives.

So now, we feel it is important to share it with you. In opening our hearts, we hope this might promote greater awareness of this condition. Perhaps it will encourage a clearer understanding of the individuals and families who are affected by it.

At the moment I feel just fine. I intend to live the remainder of the years God gives me on this earth doing the things I have always done. I will continue to share life's journey with my beloved Nancy and my family. I plan to enjoy the great outdoors and stay in touch with my friends and supporters.

clear that they realized that the president was not his usual witty, confident self.

The Reagans confronted the diagnosis with abundant courage. Nancy began to mobilize the support system that has sustained her to this day. Family members rallied round. Michael, Maureen and Ron had always been close to their father. But now, in a most heartening development, the long-estranged Patti returned to the fold, even writing an adoring book about childhood conversations with him.

The president knew very well what he could expect. His beloved mother, Nelle, had suffered from and succumbed to the ravages of Alzheimer's disease. Rather than feeling sorry for himself, however, he expressed concern for Nancy and his children. He also decided that the time had come to inform the American people—and the world—of his condition.

Unfortunately, as Alzheimer's disease progresses, the family often bears a heavy burden. I only wish there was some way I could spare Nancy from this painful experience. When the time comes, I am confident that with your help she will face it with faith and courage.

In closing, let me thank you, the American people, for giving me the great honor of allowing me to serve as your president. When the Lord calls me home, whenever that may be, I will leave with the greatest love for this country of ours and eternal optimism for its future.

I now begin the journey that will lead me into the sunset of my life. I know that for America there will always be a bright dawn ahead.

Thank you my friends. May God always bless you.
SINCERELY,
RONALD REAGAN

In the ensuing years, the president continued to play golf with old friends, to visit his post-presidential offices in Century City, and to display flashes of wit and friendliness. On one occasion, while relaxing on a park bench, he even posed for a photograph with an admiring teenager. By 1996, however, when Nancy left his side briefly to participate in a tribute to him during the Republican Party's National Convention, the president, watching the proceedings at home in the company of an old friend, was confused: he wondered why Nancy wasn't right there watching the show with him.

Eventually robbed of most of his memory, the president retained his capacity to receive and express love. Two years after his letter to the American people, his son Michael said, "He may not be able to say my name, but he knows my face, and he knows there is a hug...when I leave the house...he will be standing there, with his arms open like there's something coming, and I'll hug him."

Chapter Ten
The Legacy
of Ronald Reagan

Presidents of the United States are generally remembered by their associates and by the public for one of a variety of reasons, some mainly for having been exemplary husbands or doting parents while carrying on the affairs of state in the fishbowl atmosphere of the White House, others for their communication skills—their charm, wit, and humor—some for exhibiting grace under fire, and a very few for one courageous, visionary act that changed the nation or the world.

Ronald Wilson Reagan was a unique personality in the annals of the American presidency. He will be remembered for his steadfast devotion to and partnership with his wife of many years; his modesty—there was no pretense about him, what you saw was what you got; his great, self-deprecating sense of humor; his decency and warmth to celebrity and ordinary citizen alike—traits not usually associated with the politically ambitious; his extraordinary skill in communicating his vision for a better America; his optimism; his refusal to compromise his ideological beliefs; and for his courage and vision in redefining the balance of power in the world.

To his family, he will be revered as the adoring husband of Nancy—she has often said "My life didn't really begin until I met Ronnie," and as the concerned and caring father of Maureen, Michael, Patti, and Ron Jr. There was an added dimension of caring in Michael's case. As a youngster, he used to be upset whenever he was told how great his father was; it was as if he, Michael, had no separate identity. Then, as Michael found out more about himself, he was able to deal with his father's celebrity. Many years later, on Reagan's eightieth birthday, follow-

ing his diagnosis with Alzheimer's Disease, Michael drank a toast to him and "thanked him for having a heart big enough for the country, but also a heart warm enough to adopt a child. He brought me into his family, and loved me and cared for me."

While Reagan will go down in history as "the great communicator," without peer in articulating his strong conservative ideals and his vision of a stronger, more noble America—his style has been studied and adopted by politicians of both major political parties, not always successfully—the president possessed one attribute that cannot be taught, an extraordinary instinct for and rapport with people from all walks of life. As commander in chief, he hobnobbed with heads of state, government officials, and celebrities, but also went out of his way to relate to the public, like the time during an appearance with Israeli Prime Minister Menachem Begin when he took the trouble to shake hands with a wheelchair-bound person.

With the passing of the years, people everywhere—ordinary citizens and world leaders alike—are looking back with nostalgia at the Reagan era. Not only did the president make Americans feel better about being citizens of the United States, he railed against the brutalities of the totalitarian Soviet regime, fought for human rights, and was instrumental in bringing about the demise of the Soviet empire, not through the waging of war, but through the development and implementation of a carefully calibrated strategy based on SDI to force the Soviet Union to its knees economically.

While the Iran-contra affair posed a great threat to Ronald Reagan's presidency—and, by extension, to his legacy—his motive for signing off on the arms sale had been humanitarian: to secure the release of the hostages. And although there had been no oversight concerning the over-zealous behavior of the architect of the diversion, the president did, to his enormous credit, take steps immediately after both disclosures to provide the public with a full accounting of the misdeeds of officials in his administration.

In evaluating the presidency and legacy of Ronald Wilson Reagan, one should bear in mind that the sportscaster-turned-movie star from Dixon had not been meant to succeed as commander in chief. Yet he did, through his abiding courage in the face of ridicule; by acting on his at times controversial vision for his country and the world; by imbuing Americans with a new sense of national pride; and, most importantly, simply by being Ronald Reagan.

When Reagan left the White House in 1989, he had the highest approval rating of any president since Franklin Delano Roosevelt. Yet, as he flew west on Air Force One for the last time, he could not quite agree with the sentiment expressed by an aide, who, lifting a glass of champagne, toasted him with the words, "Mission accomplished, Mr. President." To Reagan's way of thinking, there was always more to be done to make America a better place.

As Reagan's successors have grappled with the increasing threat of Islamic terrorism, many Americans in the immediate aftermath of the horrific events of September 11, 2001, have wondered how Reagan would have responded to this new and menacing challenge. Tragically, the former president, locked in the fastness of his terminal affliction, could not offer advice or, more importantly, comfort to the traumatized nation. Nonetheless, one fundamental lesson can be learned from what has been characterized as the "Reagan Revolution:" America is at its best when its citizenry rediscover basic values and common sense, the qualities that exemplified Ronald Reagan's life, actions, and world view.

More than a decade after Reagan left office, colleagues, contemporaries and former adversaries were asked to assess his essential traits. Their observations, while of course varied, were striking in their recurring themes: modesty, human warmth, decency, wisdom, and innovation. That group, who knew Reagan as president, viewed him above all as a unifier, a political leader who had the uncanny ability of engaging people, of making them feel that he truly believed in what he said. If through Reagan's example America becomes a truly better place, its people will share in the immense satisfaction of having won one for the Gipper.

Nancy reaches out to hold her son Ron's hand as she is embraced by her daughter Patti and Rev. Wenning as she and her family have a private moment around the casket of President Reagan before the public viewing period begins at the Ronald Reagan Presidential Library in Simi Valley, California, June 7, 2004.

Chapter Eleven
In Memoriam
Ronald Wilson Reagan,
February 6, 1911 – June 5, 2004

At 1:09 p.m. on Saturday, June 5, 2004, Pacific Daylight Time—nine years and seven months to the day after he had so courageously and gracefully confided to his beloved "Fellow Americans" that he had embarked on "the journey that will lead me into the sunset of my life"—the sun finally set on the long and eventful life of Ronald Wilson Reagan, the quintessential American optimist, the so-called Teflon president, the exemplar of youth despite having been the oldest surviving president in American history.

His family and close friends had known for some time that the end was near. Several weeks before the president's death, Nancy Reagan, who has become a leading advocate of embryonic stem cell research in the fight against Alzheimer's and other terrible diseases, in a poignant announcement to the public, stated that "Ronnie's long journey has finally taken him to a distant place where I can no longer reach him." Then, in a characteristic expression of concern for others who have watched their loved ones die terrible deaths, she added, "Because of this I am determined to do whatever I can to save other families from this pain."

Then early on the morning of Saturday, June 5, the former first lady, with a terse "This is it," informed her close friend, the veteran broadcast journalist Mike Wallace, that her beloved Ronnie was in fact near death. Wallace, in turn, made the news public. Almost immediately a crowd gathered outside the Reagans' home on St. Cloud Road in the Bel-Air dis-

trict of Los Angeles to mourn the man who had cared so much for those he had served for nearly three decades that even as he confronted his mortality he offered the assurance that "...for America there will always be a bright dawn ahead."

Nancy and two of their three surviving children, Ron and Patti, were with the president as he breathed his last, his lungs destroyed by the effects of pneumonia. Michael, who had spent the previous day at his father's bedside, arrived moments after the president's death. While broad plans for the president's funeral had been in place since 1981 and updated annually, the family now began to lay out the details of the nation's final tribute to its fortieth president. It would be a state funeral, according to the tradition established on the death of Abraham Lincoln, and the pallbearers would be Michael Deaver, Merv Griffin, Dr. John Hutton, Frederick Ryan, and Charles Wick.

Despite her long ordeal and the trauma of finally losing the man whom she had famously credited with having made her life begin, Nancy found the time to thank the American people and supporters throughout the world for their concern for the ailing, and then dying, commander in chief. "We appreciate everyone's prayers over the years," she said in a brief statement.

Soon tributes were coming in from the world's leaders. From France, where he had gone to participate in D-Day sixtieth anniversary commemoration ceremonies scheduled for the following day, President George Bush, who had been wakened with the news at 10:09 p.m., Paris time, by White House Chief of Staff Andrew H. Card Jr., ordered that flags on all federal buildings be lowered to half staff. Several hours after Reagan's death, President Bush declared, "It's a sad day for America. A great American life has come to an end. Ronald Reagan won America's respect with his greatness, and won its love with his goodness. He had the confidence that comes with conviction, the strength that comes with character, the grace that comes with humility, and the humor that comes

with wisdom." Due to Ronald Reagan's leadership, President Bush added, "America laid to rest an era of division and self-doubt, and because of his leadership the world laid to rest an era of fear and tyranny."

From the campaign trail, John Kerry, the presumptive Democratic Party candidate for the presidency, said of President Reagan, "He was the voice of America in good times and in grief. When we lost the brave astronauts in the Challenger tragedy, he reminded us that nothing ends here; our hopes and our journeys continue. Now his own journey has ended a long and storied trip that spanned most of the American century and shaped one of the greatest victories of freedom."

Speaking from his summer home in Kennebunkport, Maine, George Herbert Walker Bush, President Bush's father, who served as Reagan's vice president and then succeeded him as commander in chief, observed that "He was never mean-spirited and so he set a great example. I learned a great deal from him as his vice president for eight years." Noting that they had once been political opponents, the former president said, "We became very close friends. And every Wednesday we'd have lunch alone together. And I'll never forget those lunches. There was no agenda, he didn't ask you to define different problems. It was just two people talking."

Another early opponent, President Gerald R. Ford, expressed his and his wife Betty's grief, and then said of his rival for the 1976 presidential nomination, "He was an excellent leader of our nation during challenging times at home and abroad."

Bill Clinton, whose own communications skills have often been compared to those of the Great Communicator, said that he and his wife, Senator Hillary Clinton, "will always remember President Ronald Reagan for the way he personified the indomitable optimism of the American people, and for keeping America at the forefront of the fight for freedom for people everywhere." President

Clinton also expressed his view that "It is fitting that a piece of the Berlin Wall adorns the Ronald Reagan Building in Washington."

From California, Governor Arnold Schwarzenegger, like President Reagan a former actor, expressed both his grief and deep admiration for the man he says was his inspiration, and for whom he campaigned during the 1966 gubernatorial race. "He's a big idol of mine," the governor said. "I campaigned for him. I handed out leaflets. I made phone calls on his behalf. This was at a time when I wasn't even a citizen here. He made a tremendous impact on our country."

Tributes were pouring in from throughout the world. From the United Kingdom, former Prime Minister Margaret Thatcher said that her ideological soul mate "...was one of my closest political and dearest personal friends, a truly great American. Ronald Reagan had a higher claim than any other leader to have won the cold war for liberty, and he did it without a shot being fired."

Mikhail Gorbachev, a formidable adversary during the cold war, stated, "I feel great regret. Reagan was a statesman who, despite all disagreements that existed between our countries at that time, displayed foresight and determination to meet our proposals halfway and change our relationship for the better."

From the Vatican, a spokesman for Pope John Paul II said, "The pope received the news of President Reagan's death with sadness. Two days ago, when he met with President Bush, the pope sent a warm message of best wishes to Mrs. Reagan, knowing that her husband was very sick."

Victor Orban, the Hungarian prime minister, said that "Hungary and Europe do not forget Ronald Reagan's help and the support he gave to the former Communist countries."

The media too offered praise for the late president. Many political correspondents have fond memories of—even reverence for—the man some of them had once dismissed as "That B Actor" or "The Amiable Dunce." And there were many reminiscences—not the usual polite ones offered by political pundits on the deaths of public figures. In recalling Ronald Reagan—who loved a good story and often told humorous ones to score political points—there was laughter amid the regret at his passing.

As correspondents for the major networks and cable stations covering the D-Day commemorations in France scrambled to bring viewers the latest developments in this breaking news story, they recalled Reagan's eloquence twenty years ago at the fortieth anniversary commemoration, where he had stood at Pointe du Hoc to deliver one of the most memorable addresses of his presidency.

The networks ran film clips too, of Nancy and Ronnie in the early years; of their many political appearances; of the elegantly gowned Nancy and the very physically imposing president standing with world leaders amid the splendor of state dinners; of the president and the first lady relaxing at their ranch; and most chillingly, of the president reacting as bullets fired by his would-be assassin tore into his chest.

Perhaps one of the best indicators of President Reagan's enormous popularity is that even before his death, in addition to numerous schools, roads, and highways having been named for him, the state of New Hampshire changed the name of a 5,532-foot peak to Mt. Reagan; the United States Navy commissioned the aircraft carrier U.S.S. Ronald Reagan; and National Airport, serving the greater Washington, D.C. area, became known as Ronald Reagan National Airport.

As the day of his death wore on, a hearse arrived at the Reagan residence and the president's body was removed to a local funeral home in preparation for the ceremonies that lay ahead. First, Californians were given the opportunity to pay tribute to their late commander in chief. Then on

Then on Friday, a horse-drawn caisson brought the president from the Capitol to a spot near the White House, and from there to the splendid Washington National Cathedral, where Senator John Danforth, an ordained Episcopal minister—and the newly appointed United States ambassador to the United Nations—officiated at the commander in chief's funeral service in the presence of family, friends, and world leaders. The Reverend Billy Graham had been scheduled to officiate but was not able to do so as he was recovering from a fractured pelvis. Leading the roster of eulogists was President George Bush.

Following the service, the president embarked on his final journey to California, where as a handsome young man from Dixon, Illinois, he had begun his film career; where during his marriage to Jane Wyman their daughter Maureen had been born and a beguiling infant named Michael had been adopted; where he had met, fallen in love with, and married his beloved Nancy; where she had borne Ron and Patti; where he had launched his political career; and where he and Nancy had retired on January 20, 1989, in anticipation of many more years of glorious sunsets together.

Monday, June 7, the president was taken to the Reagan Library where, following a brief service for family and friends, public viewing commenced. On Wednesday, the grieving but stoic Nancy, accompanied by Michael, Ron, and Patti, took the president aboard Air Force One on his last journey to Washington. There he lay in state at the Capitol Rotunda for two days. Throughout the nation, there was a huge, emotional outpouring as people from all walks of life gathered to express their deep affection for the president who had restored their pride in themselves and America.

Landing at the Point Magu Naval Air Station, the bereaved family went once again to the Reagan Library, where on Friday, June 11, the fortieth president of the United States, who had years earlier spoken glowingly of "a city on a hill" in defining his vision for America, was laid to rest on a beautiful, wooded hillside—at sunset.